ALL THAT WE ARE

"For additional resources, stories and content purchase the "All That We Are" Workbook and download Lion Heart's premiere mobile application "Dream & Hustle" to stay up to date with Joe Vercellino and The Lion Heart Experience. Available in The App Store.

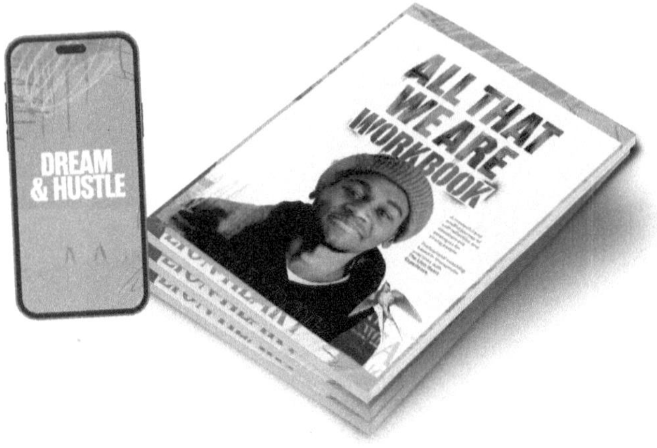

Cover design by Karl Nilsson
Front cover photo by Brian Craig
Back cover photo by Jessica Snow
Book formatting by Melissa Creative Studio
Additional Contributing Photographers: D'Isjah Lyons, Jeremiah Kanneth, Alexandra Folster.

The Lion Heart Experience
Email: connect@thelionheartexperience.com
Website: www.thelionheartexperience.com

For Eli, Selah and Amelie. I will live many stories -
being your dad will always be the most cherished
one. To Heather, my bride, what a beautiful
world we have created together. I love you.

Table of Contents

Chapters

Forward

Hey it's Tae! I wanted steal a second before you get into the book to say how proud I am of Mr.V. I met V over 10 years ago as my 5th grade music teacher and it's been special to see him continue to grow at the age I see a lot of people coasting. A perfect demonstration that our best days are ahead.

I often think about the time V and Heather got married and invited me to be part of their wedding. It was my first time seeing a marriage. Something both foreign and enriching to my life! We have enough shared experiences to keep you here forever, but one that jumps out at me is watching him get his first tattoo. Seeing him represent and wear something he lives is Honorable. The tattoo "faithful" couldn't be more fitting.

I want to thank him for setting the bar. Being a faithful teacher, friend, husband, and father.

I'm grateful to not only travel with him teaching some of the tools we use, but more importantly, see them used by people to make a shift back home.

Cheers to a Faithful Friend,
Love,

Tae Sosa

LION HEART

About The Author

The Founder and lead curator of The Lion Heart Experience, Joe Vercellino, specializes in talks, performances, and trainings in schools focused on reconnecting students and educators to a sense of self-worth and value. Known for his warmth, vulnerability, and quick connections with young people; Joe and his crew of past students bring a compelling message to schools nationwide with performances masterfully wrapped in original music, story, and visual art.

With a refreshing delivery and relaxed polish, the work of Joe Vercellino and The Lion Heart Experience both prevents and alleviates teen anxiety and depression in schools around the United States. The Lion Heart Experience reaches over 500,000 students, teachers and leaders each year and is the leading investment for suicide and self-harm prevention groups around the country.

Through dynamic school performances and invigorating training for educators and leaders, Joe Vercellino and The Lion Heart Crew tackle the toughest issues young people face from their root: a sense of worth.

Joe Vercellino was named The City of Detroit's Teacher of the Year in 2021 by Michigan's Department of Education.

PRAISE FOR ALL THAT WE ARE

"A perfect blend of deeply personal reflection with timeless wisdom, it serves as a beautiful guide for adolescents toward growth and self-discovery. *All That We Are* is a poignant and heartfelt journey for young readers as they navigate their coming-of-age experiences with insight and compassion."
Priya Rednam-Waldo LMSW MPH, Licensed Therapist and Coach

"As a clinical therapist I absolutely love the message Joe Vercellino and The Lion Heart experience has to offer kids and adults. This is a unique and powerful presentation that I believe would be a valuable asset to all schools. The messages are a wonderful lesson for our upcoming generations. What a beautiful way to empower children with positive and encouraging outlooks! 10 out of 10."
Brittney Mosqueda LMSW, CAADC, Clinical Social-Work and Licensed Therapist

"*All That We Are* and the self-guided workbook are wonderful resources for young folks to explore their personal identity and relationships. The combination of personal experiences, metaphors, tools, and songs provide meaningful examples for young people to independently connect with, learn from, and expand on."
Tatum Kline Board Certified (MT-BC), Music Therapist

"Words can't describe this life-changing experience. Joe Vercellino and his crew are so amazing and they have so much wisdom. I've personally struggled with anxiety and they have changed my point of view on it. It takes a lot of courage to shine light on such dark subjects. But this crew is so talented and they know just what to say. This was truly a masterpiece"
Chloe, Minnesota High School Student

"I cannot say enough great things about The Lion Heart Experience. Joe and his team are legit, some of the most inspiring, and real people you will ever meet. The impact that they make through their art, music, and stories is incredible, and unforgettable."
Tina Newling, Parent

"You can't love yourself any more than you know yourself, Joe."

I took a deep breath and a long look at my therapist from across the room. I don't lie down on the couch like you see in movies. I sit on this loveseat-type piece of furniture, but I sit sideways with my legs draped over the arm of the chair. I hold a pillow over my stomach, and I wear Adidas slides because I like to take my shoes off. I love this man. Jackson (my therapist) had become the MVP of my life over the course of a year. It was Jackson and I in this tiny office every week. His influence shifted my whole life, my career, all my relationships, and my marriage. His questions and insights broke into the foundations of my beliefs about the world, about people, growth, success, conflict, pain, and myself.

I felt like such a fake before starting therapy. I was burdened by the overwhelming weight of not fully being the person I portrayed myself to be. I would later learn that "playing the part without being the person," always leads to a terrible place - relationally and emotionally. You can't get up in front of thousands of students and try to bring them to a place where they might love, accept, and delight in who they are - while you silently struggle to love and accept and delight in who you are. That was me. Goodness, I feel a pit in my stomach just thinking about it.

I'm the oldest of seven children, a pastor's kid, a natural leader and nurturer of relationships, an award-winning educator, and a passionate public speaker. I am a mentor and support to a good handful of individuals, I was a proud Detroit teacher, and I started a non-profit geared toward helping kids from the city of Detroit grow. I travel with my past students like Tae and Julie around the country to talk about identity, worth, and value. Relationships are my life.

Apparently, I had neglected a very important relationship and over attended to other relationships (that concept is still new to me). I had great connections with everyone around me and what had become a fuzzy and distant connection with myself. One that was not going to be fixed by a self-care day, the spa, a massage, meditation, more money, or achievement.

I originally reached out to Jackson because I noticed a few things that presented themselves in my body.

(1) When I would be in a resting state, laying down, sitting comfortably on the couch, with my eyes closed, my mind would be racing, and even my heart. I could not relax, my mind (felt like my soul) was so burdened by frustration, disappointment in others, and anger that hid deep in my heart.

(2) Mostly on the inside, I would go from 0-100 with my emotions. What may seem like a small annoyance to most would send me spiraling into some version of a panic attack, change my breathing, and make me want to give up on life, the world, and people.

(3) I would wake up in conversation in the middle of the night angry with people that bothered me. I would (and sometimes still do) take a shower and have some type of fantasy talk under my breath finally getting to say what I wanted to say to this person. Putting them in their place.

(4) I just wanted to be in my bed, not like a depression commercial, but I wanted to be in my bed because in the middle of the night, no one needed anything from me. I wasn't performing or delivering either on a stage or for my family or in my classroom. I wasn't letting anyone down. Not even myself; that's why I wanted my bed.

This troubled me and I reached out for help. After my first session, Jackson told me that I was high performing - but struggled with pervasive depression and anxiety.

Wild. I thought depression and anxiety were for weak people who couldn't handle life.

Beginning to work through (diagnosed) anxiety and depression has been a beautiful invitation to me to learn about myself.

"What do you want for your kids, Joe?" Jackson compassionately asked me.

My kids, these tiny little humans that are somehow a mix of myself, my wife (Heather) with some sort of mystery all shaken up into this beautiful concoction - the three Vercellino children. Eli (8) comes on tour with us and will dance in front of audiences of hundreds of students. He is deeply emotional and passionate; a lot like me. He values quality time spent with us over everything. His curiosity is amusing and over the top cute. He loves to make breakfast in bed for my wife and I, something I loved to do when I was little. Yesterday he cut up a potato into squares and squeezed a lemon over it, drizzling the uncooked starch with what he thought would be the perfect morning starter – he brought it to us in bed and would not leave until I enjoyed the first bite.

Selah (6) is a princess. Selah Grace, that's her middle name. She's tiny, smaller than most kids her age. She loves to snuggle and tell you "I love you" and "you're the best." She would wear a princess dress every day if she could. I can usually find her anywhere around the house by a sort of clickety-clack sound because although she is only 6, she loves to wear heels around like her mom.

She also loves to have her hair braided and colored. She enjoys spinning around and batting her eyes. I love it when Tae Sosa grabs her little hands and spins her around in circles through the air. You can call femininity what you want but this girl was just born wanting to feel beautiful and lovely – and bring that out of people around her. Olivia, who I wrote "Glow" with, is one of Selah's favorite people. Selah launches herself into Olivia's arms to snuggle, bake cupcakes, facials and nails. Olivia and Selah sing *Rudolf the Red-Nosed Reindeer* beautifully together before bed, no matter the season. I see some of Olivia's beautiful qualities rub-off on my daughters and I'm so grateful. I taught in inner-city Detroit for almost ten years, I have been privileged to share my home and my family with some of my past students for periods of time. Living with a full saturation of my classroom and my home has been one of the great highlights of my life. Watching my children melt into the arms of people like Olivia, Julie, Arthur, Ronnie, George, Dre, Tae, Ron and Jaylin has been foundational in my experience as a father.

Amelie (4), our youngest looks like she lives under a mushroom, with straight bangs across her little forehead and hair that tucks itself before it hits her shoulders. She loves to jump to me from the bed then have me throw her onto the pillows. She tells me to "back up! back up!" to jump to me. I know she will jump only about two inches. I'll lunge to grab her, flip her around, and she will scream and smile and laugh. Even at 3 years old I can tell she loves her life and her family – maybe she loves who she is.

Returning to the moment I respond to Jackson's question, **"I want them to love who they are. "I want them to really delight in who they are, that's it."**

> **"You can't take your kids anywhere (emotionally)**
> **that you haven't been yourself"**
> **-Jackson**

(crap)

You mean I can't tell people "You're worth it! You're amazing!" leading them to a real compassionate and deep love for themselves without loving who I am? I can't fake my way into it? That's what I do for a living. I travel and speak about worth and identity and loving who you are. Here I am sitting in therapy for pervasive depression and anxiety. I could be out of a job or an entire career.

One of the questions a wise person always asks themselves is "why am I doing this, really?" with a nice pause between this and really. Deep down why did you post that? Why did you post it, really? Why did you say that, really? Why did you send that message, really? I can't take credit for that, one of my favorite speakers said that. His name is Andy Stanley. Some of my greatest achievements in life have (really) happened because I desperately needed people to see me as valuable, accomplished, and important. I (really) do a lot of things to be accepted and valuable to other people.

Can you imagine taking a breath and not having to prove yourself to anyone? Wouldn't that feel amazing? Maybe you are reading this and thinking *that's how I live my life, I'm just doing me, being myself, I don't need to prove myself to anyone.*

> Can you imagine taking a breath and not having to prove yourself to anyone? Wouldn't that feel amazing?

Maybe you take the position of a friend of mine, Elsa, who says "no right, no wrong, no rules for me – I'm free."

Modern research may suggest you and I are in deeper trouble than we realize.

While I'm writing this, at my favorite coffee shop (Dessert Oasis in Ferndale, MI) drinking an iced caramel latte. (I said that just in case you would like to remember my favorite coffee drink. I love to learn people's favorite things.)

As I'm writing this in 2023, I'm looking at data that shows that emergency room visits for mental-health related injuries in young people (self-harm and suicide attempts) went up by 31% in November of 2020.[1] Yikes. The Center for Disease Control (CDC) reports that there's 5.8 million young people suffering from anxiety and 2.7 million under the crushing weight of depression.[2]

In 2023, Over 50,000 people died from suicide.[3] More than any year on record.

Three in five teen girls report feeling persistently lonely and hopeless.[4] One in four teens have a mental diagnosis. One in 10 young people have made an attempt on their life.

Newspapers like *The New York Times*[5], *USA Today*[6], and *Forbes*[7], write articles that all say the same thing "we are the most connected and most lonely generation to ever exist."

Maybe we aren't as free or as happy as we think we are...

Good news if you are reading this – I made it through therapy. Even though I'm on my own, Jackson says that I'm doing therapy every day – because I'm serious about the things I've learned, the tools I use now, and the knowledge I have. I am a new version of myself. And I'm here to bring you into a new version as well, if you'd like. Maybe you want that?

If you find yourself on a couch laying down, closing your eyes to rest, and realize you aren't resting – there may be something for you here. If you post on your socials things that (low-key) are the furthest from where you are at as a person, there might be something for you here. If you encourage other people relentlessly and constantly give the best of yourself – you are generous and kind and always follow through for people – but also are overloaded with anger and resentment deep down… so deep you don't tell anyone about it, it might be worth spending some time together in this book. If you are thinking about your friendships and realizing they might not exist if there wasn't shock-factor humor or making jokes about each other, and you want real relationships – real relationships built on empathy, understanding, trust, relationships that lead to a real sense of belonging. If you want better connections both with the people around you and with yourself – this is an opportunity for you. If you lay your head on your pillow at night, wondering why some of the same memories keep coming back to you – it all happened so long ago yet you feel these stories echoing inside of yourself, there may be something here for you.

What you are holding in your hand are 64 stories, reflections and observations I continually come back to as a person. These are the stories, the people, the hurt, the joys and the parts of the world that sunk their hands into the clay of who I am and formed me.

If you really want to get the most out of this book – discuss it with people around and journal about it.

When I tuck in my son, I lay next to him and rub his back. I ask him how his connection was today with mom, with his sisters, with me. I ask him if there's anything going on in his heart that he would like to talk about. Then I gently pat his head and say, "how is your relationship with this guy?"

I wish I was asked that when I was little.

For Individuals, Students and Schools Using this Book

I learned how to read in college.

I have known how to process vocabulary, recognize words, read out loud, and even write papers for a long time but it wasn't until I took a class called "Death and Dying" that I learned how to read. The professor's name was Merlin. We would have to write a paper every single day in her class. Every. Day. Always a reflection on our insane amount of reading we would have to do each night. Then she would have us grade our own papers and only submit the best five to her at the end of the semester for her to grade. I actually really enjoyed the reading although it was incredibly demanding. I liked learning about how different cultures around the world deal with the idea of their own mortality. I liked learning about life-imagery and death-imagery, things we see every day that either remind us that we are alive or remind us that one day we won't be. I liked having conversations around the concept of death, not measured by a beating heart and brain waves, but as a separation from everything you hold close, familiar, and safe.

Anyway, in class we would read together. Painstakingly, together. Taking sometimes 20 minutes to get through a single page because after each paragraph, she would have us underline the main point of the paragraph. We would circle key terms that the author would use frequently. We would underline words we did not know and look up the definition – and lastly, we would write ALL

OVER the margins of the book – personal reflections, key points to remember, thoughts it would prompt in our mind. It took so long and (on top of that) there was this person in the front of the class who would have a question about everything, and they talked so slow, it just made me roll my eyes. How do you have a question after every single sentence?

Now, here I am over a decade later and I read with a pen and a highlighter. I underline main points, I circle key terms, and write "KT" next to the word. I highlight important sentences. I write personal reflections in the margins and look up words I do not know, I fold the corners of pages I want to find again, I go back and try to understand words because of the context it was used in. There's a difference between getting through a text and soaking up what the text was about.

This is not a book you just want to get through. You are going to want to soak this up, apply it to the way you process the world around you, use the lessons and reflections in this book. I'd encourage you to grab a highlighter and read this book with a pen next to you. Fold the corners of pages you really find meaningful. Circle, underline, close the book to think for a few minutes about what you read.

For Schools, Teachers, Parents and Students.

This is a book. It is not the holder of all truth. Each of the stories are written to the best of my knowledge and recollection – some names have been changed to protect the individual's identity. These stories are written to prompt thought and reflection in readers. "All That We Are" is intended for use in public education. It is good practice to review content before making it available to students or as a school resource. It is up to the discretion of the school, the school leadership and school board and policies to decide if this book is appropriate and beneficial students.

CHAPTER 1

The Original Lion Heart Story

We all have identity moments. If you are reading this, you've taken in thousands of people and places and interactions, words, and experiences – all of them have played a formative role in your life in developing how you see yourself and how you fit into the world. Even from your first entrance into the atmosphere as a baby, the way you were loved and held (or a lack of it) has formed the foundation for how you view your own importance and place in the world. Even before you could form words, your body was hitting record and filing the experience away in the deepest part of you that we call your identity. Don't confuse identity with memory. Memories are stored in your brain – moments and words and experiences that pass through your brain stem and forming pre-frontal cortex and file themselves away. Identity is what you take from the memory, it's what you learn and subconsciously apply. It's stored somewhere doctors cannot find, yet these memories and thoughts and beliefs drive us to live and some of us to die.

> Identity is what you take from the memory, it's what you learn and subconsciously apply. It's stored somewhere doctors cannot find, yet these memories and thoughts and beliefs drive us to live and some of us to die.

When you were in second grade and first heard the teacher say "go and find a partner" as they set up a class activity – you became familiar with what scientists call the fear of isolation. You felt that knot form in your stomach as you tried to figure out if you should look up or down or across the room. But you wondered, as we all do, was anyone thinking of me when the teacher said go find a partner? Did I come to anyone's mind, was there anyone in here that was hoping to get to me before someone else did? This is an identity experience. It's memory, that after it was filed in your brain, would travel someplace else into the core of your being and meaning would be pulled from it.

Do I have value? Do I have worth? Is there a beautiful future for me out there?

Identity memories are interesting, you can hit pause on them. They come back to you before you sleep or when you are waking up. You can still smell the room and see everyone around you. You cannot unhear the sounds of the feelings that filled the room. The clothing you wore still sits within the memory of your skin. You can almost zoom in and out of the memory from a birds-eye perspective, hitting pause and seeing yourself in 3rd person. If you have a memory like that, that is an **identity experience** - your brain, your heart, your soul, whatever you want to call it, has drawn meaning from that memory and it has informed the way you see yourself and your perceived value in the world.

If you have been to a Lion Heart Performance, you have likely heard the Lion Heart Origin story as it has become the platform narrative for our connections in schools around self-worth and identity. It's a story about a few moments that shifted my life forever. It's an identity moment.

When I was in 8th grade, I had not discovered or appreciated many of the gifts I now love about myself. I was not a speaker. I did not write songs or win awards. I had a few good friends. I played the trombone in band class and enjoyed the music but was not able to read the notes. I played guitar but only from watching the fingers of my teacher. I had tried almost every sport from elementary and middle school - and come to the conclusion that I just don't like getting hit, or having people chase me, or wondering if I'm going to get hurt! I was ok in academics; I could write a pretty good paper. It was really good after my dad "proofread" it and made some revisions. I did cry over my math homework multiple times, wondering how I would ever move onto harder math classes constantly saying, "I'm never going to use this in real-life." I wish I was wrong! Most of what I learned in math class I am not using in real-life. The tears though! So real :)

The girls I was attracted to were not often attracted to me, as far as I could tell. In middle school I'd do push-ups and sit-ups every night and still wonder why everyone else seemed to be so much more developed than I was, physically.

I was a very kind person though. Soft and gentle like my son Eli is. I really loved to be thoughtful, funny, and sincere. Bringing gifts to my teachers and friends was important to me. I loved to have a few of my good friends over to watch a movie and have pizza.

In 7th grade I was cut from the basketball team. Paper posted on the wall and all. Had to walk up to it and run my finger down the page to see my name not included on the roster. It was out of a movie. I remember going to the first game and seeing my friend Carson score a basket in the opposing team's hoop. *Dang, I might not be that good, but I wouldn't score points for the other team,* I thought to myself.

In 8th grade I tried out again. My coach called me over on the last day of tryouts.

"Joey (I had not yet switched to the more mature version of my name, still Joey), I'm bringing you on the team," he said confidently and warmly.

I can still see the gym in my head, I can feel the wooden bleachers with my hands as the finish, probably applied to the wood 50 years earlier wore off in chips. I was elated and optimistic! Honestly, my favorite thing that I could think of was being able to wear a jersey, wear the warm-ups, be part of the team.

"I need you to show me it wasn't a mistake to bring you on, Joey. I need you to prove to me it wasn't a mistake. I can take 14 people on the team, and you are going to be my 15th," coach said.

I walked away with a dichotomy in my hands. I was happy to be welcomed onto the team, and excited. I was also carrying a new weight of having to prove myself to someone, that I wasn't a mistake. I needed to show my coach he made a good decision.

I would only learn later in life that living to prove anything to anyone is not living.

I worked my butt off that season. For the few moments that I played I did my very best. I was one of those people that would get in the last minute or two (if we were ahead). It wasn't long before most of the season had passed, and I had not even scored a point.

We played a school called Swan Valley and somehow, I ended up at the free-throw line with the opportunity to make two points for my team. I air-balled the first shot, how embarrassing! In an effort to overcompensate I launched the ball at the backboard for my second shot banking the point and it slipped through their metal chain-linked nets. That would be my only point for the season, actually.

At the end of the season, our coach called us into the locker room after our last practice and handed out a piece of paper. I scrolled the paper with my eyes to see it was a print-out of our end of the year statistics. Fouls, steals, and points. Each team member was listed, including me, and the first column was "points for the season."

This was one of those times where if I had a pass to disintegrate into the atmosphere, I would have taken it.

My coach began reading the list and each person would stand up as he would read their statistics. I shuddered and braced myself for my name to be called. I had only scored one point the entire season. That's an average of 0.009 per game listed right next to my name.

He made his way down the roster with some of my teammate's names read first.

"Joey." I looked into my coach's eyes and could feel the conversation he had with me in the beginning of the season settling in the room.

Show me this wasn't a mistake, Joe. Letting you on the team. Show me it was a good decision...

"One point this season." The room erupted with a silent, sarcastic clap, mutters, and laughs and the unheard sound of my own self-talk.

Coach was right, it was a mistake to let me on the team.

I walked out of that practice with something that I see a lot of people walk around with. It forms them and shapes them and drives their decisions. Shame, the feeling of embarrassment that couples itself with 100% fault and responsibility. Disappointment, the feeling that it's possible that you might get picked but the people around you, if they stay long enough, will regret it. Failure, I had not delivered. I had not lived up to an expectation, I fell short, and everyone knew it. In terms of identity, it really messed me up inside.

I walked out to my dad's car, an old pink Lincoln my grandpa had given to our family. It was the size of a boat with white leather seats. I sank into the front seat and handed this paper to my dad. A piece of paper that showed the value I brought to the team, the paper that initiated the laughs and snickering that would echo inside of me for the rest of my life.

He took the paper and looked at it, he placed it on the seat and reached behind him. Pulling out a trophy. It was a small, little trophy with a figure of a basketball player on it. I looked at the name plate with my name engraved on the side.

Joey Vercellino
8th Grade basketball
Lion Heart

My dad put his hands on my shoulder. The weight of shame, disappointment, and failure weighing down on his son and he began to speak.

"All your life you will see yourself on paper, Joe. Report cards, performance reviews, end of the year statistics. It will all be measured and quantified and graphed. Coaches and bosses will tell you what value you did or did not bring."

I looked at this little trophy, the first thing I can remember with my name engraved on it.

"Can I tell you what I see in my son?" my dad said with his hand on my shoulder.

"You are the type of person the world needs, Joe. In a few weeks, the points on this paper will fade away, the record book binding will start to fall apart. Teams and coaches and players will come and go. At the end of it all, who you are - not what you do, will matter the most. I am proud of my son. You are kind and generous, you believe in other people and are warm and inviting to the people around you. The world deserves someone like you."

He continued, "This trophy is for the person that you are."

That is the story of my first trophy, a memory filed away in the back of my mind that I recall often. Now...remember I am more concerned with identity than memory. What I had drawn from the memory sinks deep into my chest.

My dad stepped into a mess of experiences and words and feelings that left me feeling like many of the young people in our country; I felt looked over, misunderstood, undervalued- he brought order and perspective. He brought warmth and sincerity. He called to the surface the things that I bring to the world that are valuable and carry a considerable amount of worth.

Especially now that I am grown up. I've been married to my wife for 10 years (a college cheerleader BTW, turns out I am able to snag the good ones), I'm a father of three beautiful children and who I am is much more important than what I do. My kids are very emotionally aware, and we talk about the things happening inside of our hearts often. I've even opened up to my son, Eli, about my anxiety and ways he can support me when he sees that I am overwhelmed and unregulated.

The rest of my life after that moment with my dad would still bring it's fair-share of hurt, confusion, heartbreak, and hardship - but at the foundation of who I am I can still recall this time with my dad to hold to like an anchor for my inner-world.

When I tell this story in schools, I paint on a 6-foot canvas. For most of my talk the canvas looks like a huge, chaotic mess. When I get to the part where my dad gives me this trophy, I connect a few blotches and lines and the audience starts to see a Lion appear on the canvas. It is quite a moment as people find themselves surprised and enchanted by the fusion of story, art, and emotion. It is always one of my favorite moments.

The takeaway is this. Today, you can help someone see a picture of themselves that they love. The CDC reports that 1-in-10 young people have tried to end their own life. For some reason, when it comes to our identity, the drops of meaning that drip onto the canvas of our life from the memories and experiences we go through; many of us end up confused, hurt, and perplexed by the picture we see. It doesn't take much to put your hand on someone's shoulder and tell them the beauty you see inside them; odds are they can't see it yet. Paint the picture.

It doesn't take much to tell someone you look forward to seeing them every day. **Paint.**

It does not take much to tell someone they are an amazing listener and that means so much to you. **Paint something today.**

It doesn't take much to stay after class and let your teacher know you see the effort they put in, or to tell your parent you know they are doing their best. **Paint.**

It doesn't take much to walk up to someone you see trying their best and look at them with soft eyes and say, "I am proud of you." **Paint something today.**

This is the essence of The Lion Heart Experience. Who knows, maybe someone reading this will be the next addition to our crew. Can we help you love the picture you see of yourself? Can we help you sort out the experiences and words and feelings that have become the foundation of our identity? Can we help offer you some perspective and order to your inner world that settles your mind and your heart?

Your best days are ahead.

CHAPTER 2

Voices

I have an alarm set for 7:00 AM each day. It goes off and I usually reach for my phone to hit snooze. I sleep with two pillows, by the way, I lay my head on one and clutch the other. I used to just sleep with one pillow until I married Heather, she put all these pillows on our bed and now I'm dependent on having two pillows - minimum. Anyway, I know there are lots of studies out there about snoozing and its relationship to productivity, or maybe that makes me a certain type of person, but it's what I do. I hit the snooze button like youtubers ask you to hit the like and subscribe button. But something about going back to sleep for eight minutes makes me enjoy the sleep even more.

When I do get up - I usually check my phone. Texts. Instagram. Email. It's also a terrible habit, it's a time waster, but that is not what I have been thinking about lately.

What I've been reflecting on is that in my first five minutes of consciousness, scrolling through Instagram I've already had 10 different people tell me the next thing I should buy, how to have better relationships, improve my liver health, the secret to making more money, everything I'm doing wrong and lastly, why Justin Bieber should be with Selena Gomez. This is not good. Too many voices in my first five minutes of the new day. Too many voices.

I walk downstairs and because I am an amazing parent, my 7-year-old is already up and has been on YouTube for an hour watching some kids that keep saying "what's up guys, guys check this out, you guys, guys smash that like and subscribe button, guys, you're never going to believe this." They pour Mentos in 20-gallon barrels of soda and unbox toys and say "guys, it's so cool" (you know the tone I'm talking about) I recognize their voices and know exactly who he is watching. So many voices.

So many voices telling me how to have a better life, what I need, what I need to buy, how to sleep better, everyone has got something to sell. So many voices telling my son Eli to subscribe and follow and comment below. He said that to me the other day, "leave a comment below." I asked him if he knew what a comment was. He was not sure but was insistent that I leave him a comment, a comment below.

> Did you know that we process over 10,000 messages a day? That's through personal interactions, our parents, teachers, friends, and others we don't notice as much like ads, texts, commercials, billboards, messaging in what we watch on Netflix, or music we listen to.

We are tuned into so many voices. Did you know that we process over 10,000 messages a day? That's through personal interactions, our parents, teachers, friends, and others we don't notice as much like ads, texts, commercials, billboards, messaging in what we watch on Netflix, or music we listen to.

That is so much information to process.

I do know this - and maybe you are with me. I want the voices I tune into to take me where I want to go. I want to seek out voices and people in my life that lead me to great decisions, healthy relationships, emotional stability. I'm not going to get there giving the first five minutes of my day to Instagram - checking to see if anyone messaged me or commented or liked a photo, then ending up on the explore page scrolling. I'm not going to get there without intentionally mapping out who's voice I need to tune into and seek out. If I don't do that, if you don't do that, I guarantee the world will fill that space for you.

Imagine what it would look like to map out what you want - for your relationships, current or future, and seek out the voice of someone who has what you want. Asking them if they might take an hour over a burrito at Qdoba to talk with you about what they've learned about relationships.

Or imagine wanting to build wealth, to make money and see it accumulate, and instead of trying to hop on the latest TikTok trend with someone who says "guys, here's an easy way to make $60,000 in a week!" and not even now if this person is for real – you seek out the voice of someone who has made some money and you ask them, "what is my first step to building wealth, would you help me?" I do not know anyone who turns down that type of honest pursuit from someone else to learn from them.

You name it. You seek out that voice.

When I was in college, I started a thing. It was just for me, but it was a thing. On Fridays I would schedule time to meet with someone who had a skill I really wanted to learn. I would sit down with friends of mine who were photographers, designers, videographers and ask if they would teach me. They always said yes, and I learned so much, they let me use their programs and equipment. I was so grateful.

I have always wanted to be a great husband and a great father. Over my teenage and college years I would meet up with great husbands and fathers, people I would not mind growing up to be like to listen to them so that I might grow up with some of their marital disciplines.

Where do you want your life to move? Are you seeking out the voices that are going to get you there? OR do you sometimes find yourself in default mode with too many voices, too many perspectives, too many suggestions, too many requests for likes and subscriptions, too many offers. Too. Many. Voices.

CHAPTER 3

We Don't Do That, Joe

Do you have a memory that keeps coming back to you? An experience that was not a big deal to people around you (they probably don't even remember it ever happened), but you - it always comes back to you. You can still feel the room, or remember what you were wearing, the sense of touch still lingers on your fingertips, or the smell of the room reveals itself in the faintest way every time you breathe in.

That's because that memory is part of your identity now. It's not just a memory. This experience that keeps coming back to you as you drift off to sleep, as you wake up, in the back of your mind when you zone out - somehow it has shaped you. Formed you like hands into clay.

The best of us, that includes you if you are reading this book, we will make our way back into those memories and figure out how they have shaped us. For myself, I have had to go back and address memories and experiences that hurt me and started a process inside of me that would eventually create patterns of thought that we now call depression. For other memories, like the one I will share with you now - it creates a sense of value, an anchor of sorts for your character and development.

When I was a kid, I was really into rugged-looking things. Clothing, books, tools, bottles, anything that looked old and worn. I knew it had a story, it had been through some things, or maybe gotten someone through something. It must have been around 10 years old that I had a fascination with old, worn books. It is possible that I was influenced by the old western movies I enjoyed at that time, where a rider on a horse carried a journal, or ledger, they would write in. It was dusty and worn, protected, and carried an unseen weight and stories of battles and dirt, restless nights, dreams, failures. Something in me longed to have something like that. I wanted a book that looked like it had gotten me through the toughest years of my life (I had yet to experience those but did not know that at the time!), I wanted a book on my shelf that looked like it had been read 50 times, carried next to me during the hardest times of my life, I wanted a book that looked like it was cried on, underlined, torn, and weathered.

The only problem is that I actually hated to read and did not have a book that got me through a hard time, I did not have a journal of vested secrets, dreams, or failures. I just wanted to look like I had a book like that.

I rummaged through my room to find something that looked like it could play the part. I found a little Bible I got when I was eight and my parents took me to church for some type of baptism or dedication. It was a tiny little white Bible that fit in the palm of my hand, the pages were super-thin with gold coating on the outside, and the words were tiny. This would do the trick for me.

I started by rubbing dirt on the cover and bending the heck out of the binding, so it was loose and stayed open easily. I hadn't actually read this book so I needed it to look like I had read each page 100 times, as it would now lay open by itself. I took different pens and underlined random words and paragraphs, a highlighter and flipped to random pages to coat the pages as if I had found mysteries and secrets to come back to. I ripped corners of pages like they had been flipped through over and over again. I made this book look like I searched for the knowledge and wisdom it may have possessed and I soaked up every drop. I took a lighter and allowed the flame to grace the cover and edges of pages as if I had fallen sleep next to this book under the night sky and the coals of a fire that kept me warm kissed the pages and cover as it lay in the dirt.

By the end of this process, I had really made this book look worn, used, pored through, and important. What started as a nice white, fresh out of the box book that fit in the palm of my hand, now looked like the prized possession of a world-traveler. The type of thing that survived with me on a desert island stranded for 10 years during a world war.

I gently set the book on my dresser, proud of what might be considered a piece of art. I was (almost) convinced of its authenticity and was sure that others would be as well.

My dad walked into the room, a tall man who just returned home from work to say hello to his creative son in his bedroom.

"What's this?" he asked me, picking up the book and flipping through the pages.

I didn't know this but about a year later my dad would end up leaving his high-status job in technology to become a pastor.

"That's my Bible," I responded, hoping that he may be convinced of its authentic and worn look.

My dad's Bible kind looked like this, actually. I would catch him reading his Bible in the mornings with his coffee. If I walked in his room early enough, I would see him crouched on the ground praying in the dark next to his bed while my mom slept. His Bible was worn from years of poring over its content, his pages were tattered and highlighted, and the margins filled with little insights of its application to his life.

He flipped through the pages, taking notes of my highlighting and underlying skills, he ran his fingers over the (now) dirty edges where I had worn off the gold lining with sandpaper.

"Joe, we don't do this." He said softly and controlled.

"We don't fake the type of people we are. It would be different if your life and your time reflected what I'm holding in my hands, but you have not pored over this book, searched its pages for wisdom, underlined things that your heart understood, or that you wanted to remember."

He continued. "If I understand correctly, you want it to look like you read a lot, this book specifically."

He looked at me with love and sternness, "Joe, be the person or don't be the person, but don't fake things – this is not a show."

I always think about that little book.

Thirty years later, my therapist, Jackson, would help me understand it in terms I would understand better.

I sat on his couch with my feet draped over the armrest after recounting this story to him.

"You can't play the part without being the person, Joe. I mean, you can, but it will always take you to a bad place. If not now, soon. If not soon, later."

"You can't play the part without being the person, Joe. I mean, you can, but it will always take you to a bad place. If not now, soon. If not soon, later."

The further the distance between who you pretend to be and who you actually are, the more it will wear on the deepest part of you. I promise.

I had just won an award for being the teacher of the year in the city of Detroit, on the same day as one of my most intense therapy session for pervasive depression. Something wasn't lining up because I did not feel like the teacher of the year. I had put in all this work and sacrifice. I was proud of my accomplishment, but somehow it didn't feel like enough. I didn't feel convincing enough. It was because at the end of the day, the motive was still to try and prove that I'm somebody and have control over the image you see of me.

Young person, I've taken the time to write about this story for myself and for you.

In our world, it is ok to play the part without being the person.

To pretend to be confident and actually be fragile and insecure.

To repost advice that we don't actually follow ourselves.

To pretend to care about justice or equality when we just care about the likes and follows that come with it.

To comment under posts about how much we love or support someone when that is the extent of our love and support.

To dance on TikTok and receive millions of views and likes and shares and still want to end your life.

To show the 3-point swish and not the 10 missed that we recorded on our phone before that.

To tell people to love themselves and live in their truth when we ourselves are home hating who we are and how we fit in the world.

We desire to not have to put in hard work, dedication, or faithfulness and want to just skip to having gone viral, become rich, or an overnight success.

We struggle to be the real version of ourselves.

Even today, my friends, I struggle with playing the part without being the person. Even me. It always takes me to a bad place. It will always leave me feeling like a fake. I always feel the urge to look more successful than I am, to appear more influential than I am. I must actively resist it or as an adult I'm still rubbing pages in the dirt to try and get you to think I am something I'm not.

Underneath all of it is a veiled attempt to try and control how people see me. Something that will, at the end of the day, exhaust me. It will exhaust you too.

Why are you really doing this?

This has become a question that I need to ask myself all the time. If what I am doing is a natural expression of who I am, my creativity, dreams, my curiosity, my belief – I need to celebrate that because much of my life has been spent to carefully craft how you see me, not how I see myself.

Sincerely, I love to read now, lots of books. I make sure to read 10 pages each morning as part of the way that I work my mind for the day. I underline and highlight, I write in the margins and carry my books around with me. I genuinely love to see my books used and worn. My favorite book to appreciate its weathering is, "Where Do We Go From Here: Chaos or Community?" by Dr. Martin Luther King Jr.

I pored over that book, in the mornings, at night, in the car, waiting for jury duty. It formed much of the way I approach my teaching and perspective on the world. It's bent and its pages are folded because I need to get back to his words. There's yellow highlighter bleeding off pages and notes in margins, the cover is ripped because of all the backpacks it's made its way in and out of.

Apart from books about growth and communication I also have my own Bible. It's worn and weathered, filled with underlined verses, wisdom to guide me, verses that re-center my sense of worth and purpose. I didn't use any dirt, or sandpaper, or fire. Just most of my life and my time. I hold these books and feel proud of myself.

I picture my dad sometimes, giving me a nod of approval as little by little my life starts to actually line up with who I actually am, not an act, not an attempt to control how you see me.

My hope for you today is that the world gets to experience a real version of you as well. I'm on the road with you.

CHAPTER 4

Heart. Soul. Mind and Strength.

Most of us are more burdened emotionally than we are physically. Don't get me wrong, life can be so draining. You are probably busy, whether you are a teacher or a student, reading this. Most of us quit because of what is happening inside rather than what is happening on the outside. It's our inner world that is shaped by encouragement, belonging, and acceptance just as much as it is shaped by disappointment, failure, or embarrassment. This inner world, or what we refer to as our identity in The Lion Heart Experience, is worth paying very, very close attention to.

> Most of us quit because of what is happening inside rather than what is happening on the outside. It's our inner world that is shaped by encouragement, belonging, and acceptance just as much as it is shaped by disappointment, failure, or embarrassment.

I have friends who track their calories in an attempt to lose weight. My wife and I sit on the couch every Sunday evening to check in on our finances together, in hopes that our investments and income can support the life we would like to have. Coaches track swings and baskets, and fouls and running times all in an effort to create data to improve the athlete they coach.

You need to track things you want to improve. Tracking creates awareness and without awareness you can't change much.

I have a pad of paper that I write in most days. Every page of this pad of paper is the same, the information I input changes. Sometimes I am planning my day and other times I am reflecting on my day – but I'm tracking. It's an emotional tracker that allows me to keep track of four areas of my life that, if I am not able to balance, things do not look good for me.

Heart. Mind. Soul. Strength.

Heart.
Before bed I ask my son if anything surprised him today. I'll ask him if anything made him happy today and if anything made him upset or hurt his feelings. At the time I'm writing this book, my son Eli is 6 years old and while I lay next to him before bed, rubbing his back and asking them these questions – what I'm doing is helping him become aware of what is happening inside his heart. Joy, loss, disappointment, delight; all of these things get stored up into our hearts and if we are going to live healthy and balanced lives – we need to keep track of what is going on inside of our heart. If I am planning my day, I will check the boxes of things that I am going to do today to take care of my heart. After all, what good is a fantastic meal or your favorite movie when you are burdened with disappointment, shame, or anxiousness? What's happening in your heart matters. Maybe you would like to track what's going on in your heart with me.

Mind.
Everything starts with a thought. Everything you see around you, good and bad, has started with a thought, which became a belief and then a creation. It's hard to comprehend that the mightiest forest truly started as a few seeds that got the right amount of sun, water, nutrients and wind to become the largest trees in the forest. I need to take care of my mind. I want to have good thoughts. I want to be smart and mature. I want to know things about people and the world and bring a valuable skillset to the people around me; whether it's in a simple drink with a friend, to a sports team or an organization I am coming alongside of. The patterns of thought, the depth of my knowledge, my interpersonal skills, learning to calm my thoughts, slow my thoughts, or redirect unhealthy thought patterns is important to me and it's important to the people around me that I am developing my mind as well.

Soul.
This word can get a little dicey depending on what your
background is. To try and keep this book as meaningful and widely
accepted in all types of settings- I would like you to envision "soul"
as the deepest part of you. The part of you that activates when you
watch a sunset and wonder how anything could be more balanced
and beautiful and artistic. Or the part of you that stands on a beach
and marvel at the water race toward your toes and retreat back
into the water over and over and over again. It's important to try
to activate this deep part of ourselves, to put ourselves in spaces
where we may realize that we are a small part of a huge world of
perfectly balanced processes that just seem to happen. When was
the last time you worked on taking your next breath? Probably
never. Your body seems to breathe in and out on its own without
you telling it to, or your heart that has been beating two weeks
after conception and it's still beating. Take yourself into the deep
thoughts and processes that happen all around us and consider
that our current difficulties, although great to us, are small when
we consider how big and broad and deep the world is.

Strength.
I run one mile a day. I'm a terrible runner. I do not like it. My jog is
very similar to a retired person you might see at the mall trying to
get in their steps because my jog is not much faster than my walk
- It's just more terrible. I get to the gym 4-5 times a week for an
hour. Moving your body, sweating a little bit, lifting heavy things,
running for a while - it energizes us and gives us new thoughts,
it floods our bodies with endorphins (I know they are there I
just don't feel them haha). Applying your strength to the day is
important both physically and mentally. Maybe you start small
and just do five pushups and a little walk around the block - but
something to say, "my day does not finish unless I have taken care
of my heart, my mind, my soul, AND my strength."

If you are looking to improve your life. Start addressing each of
these categories every day. You will notice a difference.

The LION HEART EXPERIENCE

Today's Date

i am...

☐ Planning my day ☐ Reflecting on my day

Heart

Setting aside time daily to pay attention to your emotions and you inner-world is healthy. When we can identify our emotions, we have more control over them. What's going on inside your heart today?

☐ Journaling
☐ Reflecting
☐ Identifying emotions

☐ Confessing you messed up
☐ Speaking up
☐ Expressing gratitude

☐ Having a difficult conversation
☐ Forgiving
☐ Helping Someone

Soul

Find something each day that can reach into the deepest part of who you are. Something that makes you slow down. Try to activate the part of you that feels touched when you see a beautiful sunset. What might that be today?

☐ Light a candle and sit
☐ Drink a cup of tea or coffee & feel the warm mug
☐ Pray/Meditate
☐ Slow-down

☐ Watch a sunset
☐ Put on ambient music or brown noise & lay down
☐ Find good conversation
☐ Practice breathing

☐ Catch the sunrise
☐ Cook a meal or bake from scratch
☐ Clean your room
☐ Find something that stirs you

Mind

It's time to make little decisions each day to grow. A forest once started with some simple seeds – the same is true with your mind. Let's start small, what will we do to expand our mind today or challenge our thinking?

☐ Read a few pages and reflect on them
☐ Practice a skill
☐ Learn
☐ Create flashcards for things you want remember

☐ Meet with a mentor
☐ Plan something
☐ Build something

☐ Create a checklist of things you need to accomplish
☐ Wake up earlier
☐ Listen to a podcast

Strength

Direct your ambition, both emotional and physical. Get stronger and healthier both in your body and emotionally. What part of you is going to get stronger today?

☐ Make a to-do list
☐ Set goals
☐ Go on a nice walk

☐ Work out
☐ Achieve big or small
☐ Move towards something you would like to see for yourself

My body feels...

☐ Balanced   ☐ Tense   ☐ Weighty   ☐ Calm   ☐ Achey   ☐ Low-Energy   ☐ Invigorated

How are you feeling right now?

1   2   3   4   5   6   7   8   9   10

LOW / DISCOURAGED / FOGGY   LIMINAL / LANGUISHING   SATISIFIED / POSITIVE / HOPEFUL

NOTES... Things I have learned about myself and others that I want to remember

YOU CANNOT LOVE YOURSELF ANY MORE THAN YOU KNOW YOURSELF

Emotional tracker available in the "All That We Are" workbook.

Seeds

"How many seeds do you think are in here?" I held up an apple in front of a group of students that I work with each week. They looked at me and shouted numbers through the air in the small house we meet at in Detroit.

"Five! Eight! Seven!" some of them shouted. I began to cut the apple in half and tugged out each tiny seed with the tip of the knife.

One. Two. Three. Four. Five. Six. Seven.

"Ah, Juicy," I said to my young friend in the corner who goes by the name of Juicy, "You nailed it. Seven seeds. Good Job."

I held a tiny seed on the tip of my finger, it was brown and black. Somehow the seed was able to pull off the impossible color combination. It was wet with the juice of the apple.

"Juicy, you are good with predicting numbers, can you tell me how many apples can come from this seed? If I plant this seed, how many apples will come from this seed?"

Confused faces filled the room. "How can anyone know that?" many of them muttered quietly.

I stood there taking in the moment and encouraged my students to do the same.

"In your limited knowledge and insight, you were able to predict the number of seeds in this apple."

This apple came from a tree, and within this apple is a seed... with a tree inside. My mind entered some type of deep inception-style thinking. The seed is in the fruit and the fruit is on the tree and the tree is inside of the seed inside of the fruit on the tree.

Who can know? Even in our expansive knowledge and technology, who can know how many apples could come from this tiny seed?

My friend, you may be able to predict some things in your life. You may have a plan you are following. Or maybe you are young and frankly, lost.

Yet every moment is a seed, full of beautiful possibilities for your life. Not five, not six, not seven opportunities but...infinite possibilities - stories to experience, adventures to be had, people to meet, growth to go through.

Yet every moment is a seed, full of beautiful possibilities for your life. Not five, not six, not seven opportunities but... infinite possibilities – stories to experience, adventures to be had, people to meet, growth to go through.

Opportunity Only Knocks Once

I live in Detroit, the famous hometown of the rapper Eminem. Although I was a pastor's kid, and according to my father, Eminem was basically equivalent to Satan himself, I would still find ways to listen to some of Eminem's music as a kid. I remember when his explosive song "Lose Yourself" came out.

You better lose yourself, in the music the moment you want it
You better never let it go
Cause you only get one chance, do not miss your chance to blow
Cause opportunity comes once in a lifetime...

Have you heard the song? It's hard not to nod your head to that one. ;) The song makes you feel like you can play basketball in the NBA when in reality, you can barely hit the backboard.

My second year into teaching, I had this small group of boys that I would get together with before and after school. We would use the buckets, trash cans, and assorted pieces of donated drum kits to weave together the underground sound of Northpointe Academy. It was rugged and raw and beautiful to me. These boys would end up at my wedding a few months later and be the first to hold my son, Eli – when he was born 2 years later. This was a special group, not only because of the music but because of the faithfulness we showed to each other.

Out of all the people that our group could have caught the attention of, I got a call one day from Honey Bunches of Oats. Yes, the cereal. "We're feeding America!" They say in all of their soulful and American heartwarming commercials handing bowls of cereal to construction workers on the jobsite and accountants while punching numbers at the office.

"Yea, we want to feature you guys on a cereal box, we love what you're doing together." The producer told me. "We want to get a video crew out there to Detroit and do some filming with you all."

I was surprised, caught off guard, and also honored that a cereal company had expressed interest in this tiny rap group that consisted of some kids from the city and random white dude in skinny jeans and Justin Bieber hair.

Nevertheless, it happened. The video crew came out and brought all their sound and lighting equipment with them. Fog machines and speakers, producers, and audio techs. They fed us and made us feel so special on the set while they filmed content for this cereal box.

At the end of the day, the producer was walking down the steps of the school with me.

"So, Joe, what's the plan? Like five-year plan here? What if someone asks you that and you have to sell them on what you are doing right there?"

I stopped and pondered on the steps for a second.

"Like, what if they just say hey, this guy is just building a boy band and they pass you up. You got something great here, you need to have a good answer, opportunity only knocks once..." and he hopped into his car and drove away.

I stood there in front of my empty school as the last bit of sunshine peaked through the buildings in Detroit. I needed an answer, opportunity only knocks once. If I wanted to be something, If I wanted this group to be something, I could miss it all in a moment.

Then a small voice, almost inaudible met my frantic thoughts.

> Opportunity does not knock once in a lifetime. It does not pass you by. It presents itself every day in all types of moments.

It's not true.
In my experience, opportunities come all the time – big and small.

Opportunity does not knock once in a lifetime. It does not pass you by. It presents itself every day in all types of moments. You may take advantage of the opportunity; you may miss it. Neither defines you as a success or failure.

When you believe that you only have one moment and you better not miss it, it will make you live in fear and living in fear is the worst.

Friend may this thought bring you comfort. My hope is that when opportunity knocks that you are ready to soar – I also hope that you dig in deep and think about who you are, what you want and what you are building – and do not let "opportunity" overshadow the importance of just building something humble and beautiful.

I travel now, speaking and performing in schools all around the country. One of the boys in that cereal box shoot is now one of my best friends. At the time he was in 5th grade and his name is Tae Sosa. I was a second-year teacher trying to figure out who I was as well.

Opportunity knocks, and knocks, and knocks.

CHAPTER 7

The Tree is Going to Die

I had the most intriguing conversation. I was talking with my aunt about my cousin who was in 5th grade at the time. With her class, they had built a terrarium; a large transparent box meant to keep in moisture, focused light, and create the ideal environment for plants to grow in dirt - kind of like a mini-greenhouse.

They grew lots of plants on the inside. There were flowers, and produce, vines, and even a small tree - all of which started from seeds.

Everything thrived. Sprouts reached toward the ceiling in the perfectly nourished dirt. Leaves and buds began to show. The smallest versions of cucumbers and beans were visible. The tiny Oak tree started to tower over the other plants even in its infant form. It was hard to believe that this tiny tree would one day have thousands of bright green leaves - all it takes is time.

Everything was going perfectly until one day, my cousin looked in her terrarium and noticed the tree was looking a little withered, not standing tall as it once was. Thinking this would be an easy fix, she gently poured some water near the roots and moved the terrarium closer to the window for some classic sunlight. Surely this would do the trick, every other plant seems to improve if you have three things covered (1) water (2) sunlight (3) dirt. Some plants don't even need dirt to grow - so this oak tree had no excuse in her book to be discouraged.

The next day came, and the tree was no longer towering over the other plants, it's leaves withered and tiny trunk bent towards the ground as if it were defeated. Why? How frustrating to watch a plant...dying? Could it be dying with all of the water and sunlight it needed? Even the dirt was infused with compost to create the ideal living environment for these tiny green factories to thrive.

"The tree is going to die," a voice behind her gently, but confidently shared. Her teacher moved closer to the enclosure and opened the door, reaching in to lift the small trunk off the ground that seemed to be looking worse by the minute.

"What do you feel in here?" The teacher asked, reaching his hand in the glass box.

"It's kinda hot, I guess," she responded. Thinking that maybe the concentrated heat and moisture was too much of a rain forest environment for an oak tree.

"Reach in again, what else do you feel?"

As if trying to grasp some type of invisible magic or unseen intruder she said. "I really don't feel anything?"

"That's why the tree is going to die," the teacher responded. "You feel no wind."

"You can grow a cucumber, or beautiful flowers in that terrarium - but a tree will not survive without wind. The resistance of the wind pushing against it forces the plant to plunge its roots deep down into the soil. A small tree trying to stand tall in a rainstorm is actually...good for the tree. It is for its benefit and health and life. Without the wind, without the resistance, without any adversity this plant will not force its roots down deep and it will die in the process."

I cannot read this story without considering my own life. I do my best to avoid wind and resistance and I try to minimize adversity. Could it be that I should be considering myself when I look at this tiny tree and its potential to grow up strong to eventually tower not over flowers but houses?

Here's the takeaway. You need the wind. You need the resistance. You need the adversity. I do too.

Through facing "wind" in life, like difficulty. Failure. Disappointment. Embarrassment. Loss. It forces us to dig deep and send our own roots down into the ground in hopes that we will one day stand tall.

Through facing "wind" in life, like difficulty. Failure. Disappointment. Embarrassment. Loss. It forces us to dig deep and send our own roots down into the ground in hopes that we will one day stand tall.

Do you know what's down there? When you force your roots and emotions and mindsets to dig deep? When you are not overcome by a storm in your life but are able to look around and take notes of what is affecting you, naming it, choosing your response and holding yourself together?

Confidence. Strength. Resilience. That's what is down there.

The chance to move forward in life and begin to tower over what was once difficult and say "because of the wind, because of the resistance and adversity in my life, I am able to stand tall and say - you too will make it through"

The
LION HEART
EXPERIENCE

@lionHEART TEACHER #Trust
TESSA lion heart

The
LION HEART
EXPERIENCE

 **thelionheartxp**

View insights

Boost post

 Liked by **k.m.driessnack** and **43 others**

thelionheartxp Lion Heart Crew getting ready to head out tomorrow! Kicking off the 2018-2019 tour in Lowell, MI #lionheart #lionhearttour #identity... more

View 1 comment

September 19, 2018

The
LION HEART
EXPERIENCE
FOR THE LAST,
THE LOST,
THE LEAST & THE
LOOKED OVER
BASED IN DETROIT, MI

FARGO

The
LION HEART
EXPERIENCE

CHAPTER 8

Dichotomous

Sometimes at schools, students ask for our autographs. We sign shoes and paper and notebooks and foreheads and arms. It's always a bit funny to me because where we are from, no one would ask for our autograph because no one cares. There are always some autographs that I never forget though, it's when students pull up their sleeves for me to sign their forearm and I see all the scars from them slicing their skin through self-harm.

I remember talking to a young person who would cut. She told me "When I do this, at least I can identify this pain, that helps me, because the pain I feel inside I can't identify easily. I know where this pain is coming from because it's self-inflicted, the rest of the pain I carry daily – I don't know how to address it, heal it, confront it, untangle it, or name it."

We are the freest and the most medicated that we have ever been as a country. We live in a world where we are encouraged to say what we want, speak our truth, do what you want, express, be who you want, just do you.

Sounds a lot like freedom, right? I don't mean to bash Elsa from Frozen; I know I already mentioned her earlier. "No right, no wrong, no rules for me, I'm free." It may be a form of freedom, but it's a dichotomous freedom.

Dichotomous means that you need to hold two things that seem to be opposing and supporting each other in the same hands. In your right hand you hold the idea that we live in one of the most expressive, inclusive, and accepting cultures in the world. In your left hand you hold the staggering rates of anxiety, depression, self-harm, and suicide.

If we are so free, why are so many people hurting so bad on the inside?

Dichotomous is a word I use frequently when I speak - mostly because I run into dichotomies all the time and so do you.

This is not the only place we live with dichotomies. Have you ever been delighted and sad at the same time? Maybe you broke up with someone, you knew it was for the best, but it sucked so bad, and it hurts. Or you are really going to miss someone - but you also would like to be alone and have some personal space.

Did you know that living with these dichotomies is part of what makes you human? We can hold two different emotions at the same time and somehow, they swirl together like two flavors of ice cream in a soft-serve cone. Vanilla and chocolate.

CHAPTER 9

5:30 AM

Before you get any ideas.

No, I am not (currently) that guy who wakes up at 5:30 AM to get in a workout, read, journal, meditate, start an LLC contribute to my 401k, take my multi-vitamins and record a podcast before my kids wake up. But my alarm does go off at 5:30 AM and probably not for any reason you might think of :)

When I was in high school the first alarm was set for 2:30 AM. Not for pushups. But each night, while it was dark and the house was quiet and the air outside was still - my alarm would quietly go off to bring me to consciousness even though I would be going to back to sleep less than 120 seconds later.

When my alarm sounds, these are the thoughts that go through my head.

(Alarm Sounds) (I reach over to turn it off)

(Breath)

Internal Thoughts: My bed is so warm and cozy, I love my bed, I'm so delighted to know that I have 4 more hours of sleep before I have to wake up at 6:30 for school - This is the best.

Crazy, right? Isn't the feeling of waking up and realizing your alarm isn't going off in five minutes the best? In fact, waking up in the middle of the night thinking you are nearing morning then checking your phone to see it's the middle of the night.

I love that feeling. I love it so much that I schedule it into my nightly rhythms. I know it's probably better to sleep through the night without interruption but I have to have it. Waking up at 7:30 AM when my 3-year old is standing next to my face asking if I could fetch her chocolate milk, wishing I could just have five more minutes, I have to get that feeling on my own.

Waking up in the middle of the night to just soak for a minute in delight and comfort and control when the waking world seems to drain you of those rather than fill you, I need to go grab that feeling even if its just for a few moments of consciousness.

You might be wondering what my wife thinks of this practice/habit. She has been hearing impaired since she was a child and regularly doesn't hear her own alarm - a good excuse to lean over and give her a kiss or arm scratch when I hear hers go off ;)

Now, what would this story have anything to do with you?

Filling up your heart with gratitude is an excellent practice. A Harvard study of two groups, one that reflected on daily irritations and one that reflected on daily gratitude offered staggering results in their mental and physical well-being.

I wake up to be grateful for a second. If you know me like my family does or The Lion Heart Crew does - I definitely tend to lean more towards irritation, judgement and annoyance.

This little alarm in the middle of the night helps me bring a touch of gratitude in my life when I naturally struggle to show it. My bed is so warm, I love it. I get to sleep longer, I'm grateful for the time. No one needs anything from me, I'm in control and I get to close my eyes again.

See you at 5:30.

CHAPTER 10

The girl on my bus

Joey.

That's what people have called me for most of my life. Except today. My bus driver doesn't know my name as I step on to the big orange bus from my first day in Kindergarten. Lurching my legs forward to step up on to the aggressively giant steps for my first ride home from school. I can still hear the bus doors opening while the greasy metal levers swing back and forth. My bus driver, who I will later learn is a sweet lady named Helen *(a perfect name for a bus driver)* feels intimidating. She's kind of gruff and wears reflective sunglasses so you never know if she is looking at you or not.

To be honest, I just want to get home. Kindergarten is so brand new, everything is different. It's not like home. There's lots and lots of new people, new expectations, I need to remember where to sit specifically on the rainbow carpet. My teacher Mrs. Bober is very kind and sweet, like the grandma. She's old but I feel comforted by her presence.

On the bus, older kids find their claimed spots in some sort of hierarchy that I do not understand yet. Big kids are in the back, smaller in the front. I do not want to sit in the front row, so I tuck myself against the wall and peer out the window a couple rows back. If you stepped onto the bus, you would not even see me I was just a tiny little kid.

The buses all left the school together in a gravely migration out of the school parking lot. I see what may be an illegal amount of smoke puffing out of the bus exhaust pipe in front of us. This is Poseyville Road, the road I live on, my house is just a few miles away and I am good at being patient as the bus stops, a child exits, gets motioned to walk across the road and we move on to the next stop. Mine is coming up soon. I am anxious to get home to something familiar. I want to see my mom.

Though while approaching my house, the bus begins to speed up, growling under my feet like a bulldozer. My bus drivers' eyes set on the road before her. *Does she know I'm here? Does she see me? My house! We are passing my house!* My internal shouts echo around my whole body, dread drops on to me like a blanket, but I can't manage a shout or even mutter a word. I watch my house wiz past. I know my mom is in there, did she see the bus go by? Does she know they missed my stop? Hot tears of nervousness fill up my eyes. I can't walk up to the front crying, that would be embarrassing. I just sit there; kids pass me and hop out stop after stop. I'm further from home than I've ever been, I don't know these roads, I don't know these houses, the bus has turned, and I don't even recognize the street names. There are only a few kids left and I swear the sun is going down.

I sniffle and wipe my nose while a girl from the back of the bus drifts towards the front for her stop. She has big curly hair and freckles. Probably the biggest I have ever seen. She's a fifth grader. She looks my way and says "why are you crying?" in a gentle and concerned voice...

"my house, the bus missed my house," I break down in tears finally saying it out loud. The words cross over my lips and saying them makes me feel more lost than ever and I have no control. "I just want to get home," I say through muffled tears and sobs. "She missed my stop. I was supposed to get off so long ago..."

"Ms. Helen! You missed this little guy's stop! Turn the bus around, you missed his stop, you missed his house!"

I'm 36 years old writing this in a Panera Bread shop in Rochester,

Michigan. I still feel like crying as I recall this story. Not because it is sad to be lost and far from home. Because it is beautiful to feel found.

Ms. Helen pulled over the bus and came back to comfort me, telling me she had no idea I was there and would get me back home soon.

"My name is Liz," The girl on the bus said to me quietly sitting down. Her presence soothing my soul.

Liz.

You saw me. You saw my tiny little kindergarten body and my tears, and you said something. You stopped the bus and told it to turn around. I can't forget you.

Why might I share this story with you, my young reader. Well, because there are many people on a bus wanting to get home. Because there are many of us wondering If anyone can see how lost we are pressed up against the wall looking out the bus window. Because too many of us well up with hot tears alone because we missed our stop, or we messed up, we didn't speak up when we were supposed to. And now life has taken us so far from home that we see roads and places we were not meant for. We are so far away.

But when someone like Liz walks by to notice us, we never forget them. They get the bus to turn around and sit quietly with us until we get home.

CHAPTER 11

A Piece of Mail

When I was in college, I lived in a house of nine guys. We all had our own rooms and shared two bathrooms- I'm still not sure how all of that worked out. On Monday nights we would all meet for a couple hours in the living room and talk over ways that we were growing, things we were learning, and found ways to support and encourage each other as we moved through life.

It was the first time I think I really tasted what would be considered brotherhood. I haven't really felt anything like it since. Brotherhood, or to make it more widely accessed, real belonging. These were people who looked forward to seeing me, missed me if I wasn't there, people who delighted in who I was and valued what I had to contribute to the house we were in. Four nights out of the week we would cook dinner with a partner in the house we were paired up with, we did it for nine guys and two guests each night for under $25. We got really good at finding deals and eating on a budget. I always did pasta because you can feed a lot of people with that, or the local bakery sold day-old bread really cheap, and I'd make toasted sandwiches. It was at one of these meals that a friend invited this beautiful girl over, named Heather, who would infatuate me, and I would end up marrying her. We are coming up on 10 years together now and have three beautiful kids and an even more beautiful life. I love to be faithful to Heather and experience her faithfulness as well.

The house had a leader, his name was Grant, he was a couple years ahead of me in college and he initially invited me to be part of this house. To be invited in meant so much to me – never underestimate how powerful it is to invite someone into something great. I lived in this house and contributed to it; I liked to learn from Grant. One day I got a letter in the mail, stamped, and addressed to me. It was from Grant, who lived about ten feet from me down the hall.

> One day I got a letter in the mail, stamped, and addressed to me. It was from Grant, who lived about ten feet from me down the hall.

I opened the letter and read it to myself, a little confused as to why he would write a letter, address it, and mail it from our house, send it through the mailing system just to have it delivered right back to where it left, but in different hands. In the letter he told me that he loved what I added to the house, strengths he saw in me, and that he believed in what he saw in me as a leader. It was so kind.

I knocked on the door to his room (he wasn't always in his room; he just was at this time) and thanked him for the kind letter. I asked him why he didn't just slip it into my bag, leave it on my dresser, or just tell me those things since he saw me every day.

He said that he likes to do things intentionally to slow down. Do things to slow himself down. It's easy to send a text, shoot an email, or a DM. But he wrote with a pen and piece of paper, went at the pace of his thoughts and handwriting, he folded the paper and slipped it into an envelope, addressed it to me – stamped it and put it in the mail.

That experience made an impact on me.

Each year, ever since that experience, I send letters out on my birthday to people who have made an impact on me. People who love like I would like to love others. People whose words still ring in my ears and shape my being. People who have been kind and faithful to me. It's good to make yourself slow down. Take the long way. You may discover something beautiful along the way.

A Dose of Awe

I ate an apple the other day. Personal note, I do not like apples or bananas. I think it's mostly a texture thing, the goopy texture of a banana is so gross and the sound of biting into an apple makes me cringe. I promise I'm not high maintenance! I did eat an apple though, probably because I wanted to be healthy and that is the first go-to move for most of us.

I decided to cut the apple and not eat it like I'm Johnny Appleseed or something. How many seeds are in an apple? Maybe 5-7? I held one of those seeds in some type of cinematic, sentimental moment of awe knowing the power to grow an entire apple tree was in my hand.

I thought to myself, the apple was on a tree with the seed in the apple and the tree in the seed in the apple is in my hand (That has to be one of the worst written sentences but that was the best I could do). I was having what scientists would call a dose of awe.

The power of endless apple creation, begging to be shoved into the dirt was looking at me from my palm. Same for all seeds, cherry pits, avocado pits, kiwi seeds, you know those little helicopters that spin to the ground in the fall from maple trees, or pinecones - how does nature recreate itself like that?

Did you know that when females are born, they are born with

every potential egg that can be fertilized later in life already inside them?[8] As a baby? So that means that while Amelie (my daughter) was in my wife's body, that my wife had a person in her body with the potential to create another person already there! I'm in awe and I had not even held her tiny life yet.

There's a lot of talk around being able to inhabit the planet Mars. It could happen one day. Look around though, there's air to breathe on this planet. Anywhere on the planet. We have water and forests and icecaps and deserts all on the same planet. We are close enough to the sun to stay warm and experience seasons while also not so far that the entire planet would freeze to death. We have precisely the perfect amount of gravity pulling on us that we stay on the ground and don't fly into space. Isn't that amazing? The balance of it all.

Isn't it amazing that you are reading this book not thinking about the fact that you are breathing. Your body is doing it on its own. And your heart, your heart has been beating since you were two weeks old. I'm talking about your heart that starts forming and beating two weeks after you were conceived. Look at you now, still in motion. It's amazing. Keep it up.

> Isn't it amazing that you are reading this book not thinking about the fact that you are breathing. Your body is doing it on its own.

A dose of awe[9].

Why do we need these moments? A dose of awe. A spoonful of awe. A small intake of realizing the world is so big and complicated and balanced and beautiful.

We need these moments to ground us, offer us perspective, and send us into each day with a sense of gratitude to somehow play a small part in it all.

Experiencing, seeking out, and celebrating these moments will lead you to a new version of yourself, I promise. Seek out a dose of awe every day.

CHAPTER 13

"You're A Good Man, Joe"

I have a verse for a song that has not yet found a home. It's living
in the voice-memo hotel of my phone that features all the tiny
whispers of melodies and lyrics that descended on me in the middle
of the night. I'll grab my phone off the shelf next to my bed and
sing them softly into my phone, so they aren't lost when I wake
up. The voice memos sound funny because I do not want to wake
up Heather who is sleeping next to me. Other voice memos are
recorded in the car, fresh out of the shower standing in a towel,
sitting at the piano in my living room. It's fun to look back and hear
the earliest origins of a song that is now complete and part of the
Lion Heart catalog on Apple Music or Spotify.

Anyway, I've got this line where I'm talking about growing up.

*"...my daddy was a preacher **and my momma** she could teach ya
anything about the heart, wish I could keep it in a box."*

My mom is the emotional compass and foundation of all of my
sibling's ability to make others feel valued. All seven of us. Even
when I was young, I loved to get my friends around my mom
because she is so good at making you feel heard, understood, and
valued. She has an eternal optimism and belief in people. Even
times that I deserved judgment, my mom offered me grace and an
invitation to be more, instead of slamming me back into my place.

I drank chocolate milk out of a hollow noodle straw once, at an

Italian restaurant when I was probably 11 years old. It started to get a little soggy after about 20 minutes. I remember this noodle straw and chocolate milk because I was on a date with my mom, very special times that both my parents committed to sharing with my siblings and I each month. We would get to pick something special to do with our parents (movies, dinner, shopping) and have the chance to have mom or dad to ourselves for an evening to do something that we enjoy. I love that my parents did this. Apart from it making us feel very special, it helped to set a standard for my brothers and sisters of the type of people we would end up wanting to share our life with. They had to at least be as intentional as my dad and as understanding and gracious as my mom.

In this specific memory in my head, I went to have Italian food with mom, I drank chocolate milk out of a straw, and I got to pick out new pencils for school that had NFL players on them. I loved this time with my mom.

Through the course of my life, sitting with my mother to connect has been the foundational emotional experience for being able to operate in the soft skills that make the biggest difference in life. Compassion, Empathy, Understanding, Forgiveness, Conversation, Clear communication – in all the seasons of my early life to now, from bullies to break-ups, times of loss and times of opportunity, marriage, career shifts. My mom has slowly, diligently, and in a beautiful pattern, always positioned herself to bring the value of the relationship to the forefront.

Even while I'm writing this at 35 years old, I had said some things to one of my siblings a few days ago that was judgmental and harsh. It naturally wasn't received well; I was wrong, and my natural instinct was to just pick up my toys and go to another sandbox.

She reached out to me again, in a time where I deserved judgment - with encouragement to bring the value of the relationship to the forefront and I did, "You're a good man, Joe. It's worth it to do the hard work to keep the relationship strong."

"The Good is always in you, Lion Heart Just brings it out."
Tae Sosa

I am Nature

I'm not a nature guy. You will not find me camping in a tent and I will only go hiking if I can return to the hotel after our hike. I love to learn about things you can eat in a forest, but I do not have a ton of interest in going out to find those things. I remember as a kid I was on a kick of discovering plants you could eat in nature, and I found a book at the library that said you could use dandelion leaves as a salad. They were gross so I just covered them in ranch and somehow felt I was messing up the whole connection to nature with my Hidden Valley salad dressing. I do LOVE to learn though; I love to learn and observe and soak things in.

Ever heard of the bee pollination business? Imagine you are a farmer; you have a field of flowers and a truck full of bees shows up next to your field. You can hear the bees buzzing in the truck, vibrating. You pay the beekeeper for their pollination services and the beekeeper opens the containment and all the bees fly out and pollinate your field, a few hours later they all return - All of them. How?

Because somehow, these bees have elected, vowed their allegiance and entire being to a queen bee, and they will go and return to where that bee is. Insane.

What's your favorite part about nature? Is it a sunset and the brilliant oranges and yellows, reds, and purples that spread across the sky right before the sun dips down? Is it standing next to a huge body of water knowing there's a whole world of nature happening beneath the surface? Plants and fish and habitats, ecosystems, and food chains dependent on each other's survival? Maybe it's watching the tide come in and go out repeatedly wondering how the water moves like that.

> What's your favorite part about nature? Is it a sunset and the brilliant oranges and yellows, reds, and purples that spread across the sky right before the sun dips down?

For me sometimes it's thinking about how water evaporates from a lake, goes up into the sky, accumulates in a cloud, the cloud gets heavy and drops the water back down on the earth, and the cycle repeats itself.

We often go out to see nature, we watch the seasons come and go. That tree outside your house is full of green leaves in the summer. In the winter the tree looks lifeless and bare, yet somehow, alive? Like for hundreds of years alive. Then in the spring buds appear and take it back into is beautiful green existence.

We watch nature on TV, documentaries on sharks and polar bears. Yet, for most of my life I have unintentionally neglected the fact that I am also part of nature.

I am part of nature. Which means I am also subject to what I see in nature. Things like seasons and processes beyond my control.

Let me break this down a little bit. We imagine that our life is kind of like this graph on the next page. That as time goes by, as I gain years and experience, so should I also accumulate satisfaction, happiness, achievement, and success. Yet, I look outside my house and see a tree that is green for a few months, then the same leaves are yellow and red as they fall, in the winter the tree looks lifeless, and in the spring life appears again.

I am convinced that if I am to have a healthy perspective on life I must embrace that, I too, go through seasons both on a micro and a macro level. Seasons of life and abundance. Seasons of loss and hurt and things being stripped away. I will have seasons of new beginnings even though I am the same tree, I mean person.

I am part of nature and subject to its rhythms as well. Somehow, I am breathing in and out similar to the way the ocean pushes water in and pulls it back out to sea. I accidently cut my foot and over time my body heals the wound by itself.

What should this cultivate inside of us. Perspective? Yes. A dose of awe? Yes.

This thought, in its most mature form, should cultivate a sense of self-compassion. Or in simpler terms, the ability to take it easy on yourself. To offer compassion inward in the same way we offer it to others. To ease up on the incessant need to achieve and accomplish and breathe. To participate in the tide of the ocean. Or to notice that after a storm, their seems to be a brilliant sunset and so to may you experience that. Or to recognize that I am in a season, and I will soon move to another. Self-compassion is so powerful. My hope is today that as you observe the world around you, that you might embrace your privileged place in nature as well.

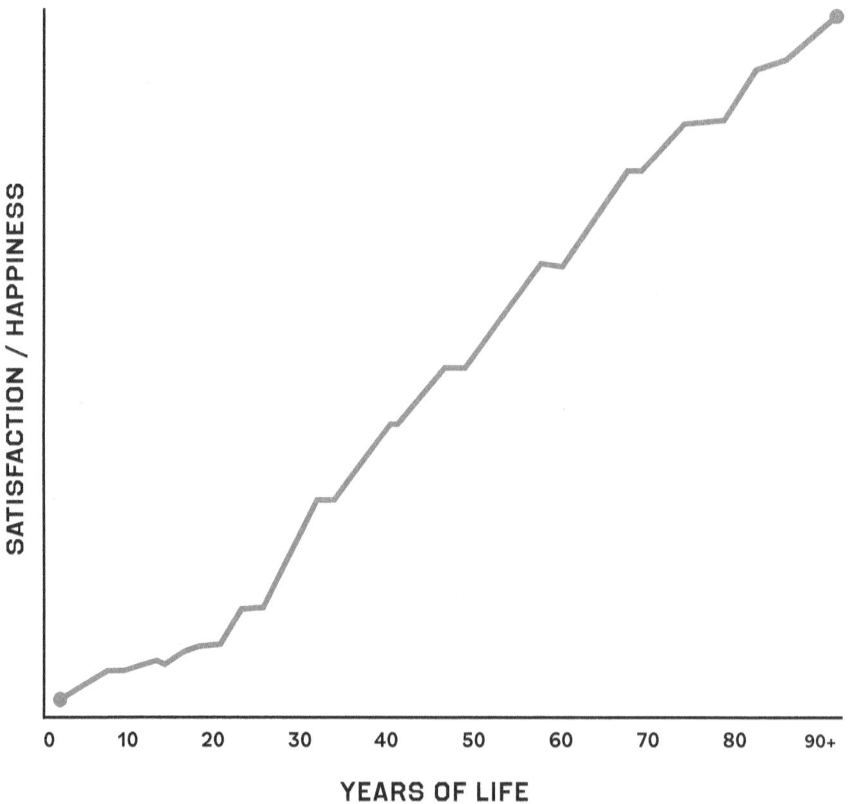

CHAPTER 15

The Timeline

My therapist, Jackson, asked me to create a timeline of my life. Those were his only instructions. My mind went back and forth on how I was supposed to organize it. By birth years? Major accomplishments? He just told me to include what I thought was necessary and to write the first things in my mind. I drew a horizontal line across the page with the first tick mark being in 4th grade. In 4th grade I found out this girl liked me. I really liked her a lot and for as much as I could gather at that age, she was out of my league. Her name was Annalise. She came over to my house once, I was really good at making no-bake cookies. I was so elated and delighted she was there. I remember stirring a cold stick of butter in the pot because I forgot to turn on the stove. We would ride my family go-cart around the yard, I remember stopping it to ask her if she got the note I had passed to her at school through other people.

"I did get your note," she said through her helmet with a cute smile, and I hit the gas on the go-cart like it was my only time I would ever get a chance to impress someone with my driving.

At the end of 4th grade, I remember sitting on the bus and a friend of mine pointing out the window saying, "that's who Annalise likes now," pointing to a little kid walking out of school - I sized him up in my head, confused on what this person offered that was better than what I offered Annalise. I didn't get it. When did the feelings stop and did I do something wrong? It was my first time feeling left behind. I reflect on that memory a lot, actually. I feel like it was the origin experience for me that launched a very real fear for me that no matter how good a relationship feels, they would probably end up leaving me and I wouldn't see it coming.

First tick mark.

I continued trying to flow and not over think this.

Fifth grade recess. Tick mark.

I was on the playground in a football game. I remember being surprised I even got picked to play because my skills were not quite up to par in football. I was happy to be out there, and it was more exciting because there was a bit of a crowd that had gathered to watch. It was dusty and dry, probably close to summer. The play started and someone tossed me the ball, I took off hoping to just gain a few yards and run out of bounds until one of the opposing players ripped the ball from my hands knocking me to the ground. He ran for a touchdown, and I remember everyone chasing him and I felt so embarrassed he took the ball right out of my hands and now I was laying on the ground.

Second tick mark.

Event after event presented itself on my timeline - a few minutes later I was all the way into my thirties and I made another mark, this was the time I painted a canvas in front of the entire school that I taught at and completely botched the lion on the painting that would become the centerpiece of every performance we've done. The eyes were crooked, face warped. It was terrible and humiliating. I felt like such a fake. That whole weekend I wanted to crawl in a hole and never show my face. Who would ever take me seriously? I can still see the whole performance in my head.

I continued this timeline of my life, making tick marks and small descriptions. I had birthdays but never included them in the timeline. I made major accomplishments like graduating, getting my first teaching job, but none of those seemed to make the timeline that was taking shape here. Marriage, kids...none of them included on the timeline of my life.

Each event I felt like I should include was, in some form, about loss, being misunderstood or embarrassed.

Apparently when I document and organize my life in my own mind, it is through the lens of loss and being left, being misunderstood. This is how I see life - this informs my decisions, my fears, my goals, my investments, my relationships. Everything. It also helps me offer myself compassion and creates awareness because operating out of fear is a bad way to move through life.

> Apparently when I document and organize my life in my own mind, it is through the lens of loss and being left, being misunderstood.

I tried this activity with another group of young people and gave them the same directions; **Make a timeline of your life.** Each person shared their timelines - it was so interesting to catch on to the patterns and wiring of each person as they presented. Some gave a clear picture of their life, but it was through the lens of emotional pain like mine. Others presented their timeline, and it was focused on their family relationships and health. Some presented their timeline, and it was focused on the different places they lived during their childhood and heavily informed their desire to have a single place to call home.

You probably know where this is going.

Create a timeline of your life. Don't overthink it. Share it with someone and ask them if they see any patterns in the things you chose to document.

CHAPTER 16

Five Years

Who will you be in five years?

Dang. That's a long time. What were you doing five years ago?

I have a young friend who graduated High School and went to college to play football. He was talking to me about how, one day, when he makes it to the NFL – he would come back and give to the community, mentor the youth and donate athletic gear.

I love this young man, but I didn't believe him. Here's why.

If generosity is not part of your life now. It will not be part of your life in five years.

If you want to know who you will be in five years you need to do nothing more than look at who you are now and increase the intensity and scope. I suppose that for some of us that should be encouraging, for others, challenging.

Let me offer some examples: Mentoring the youth someday is a great ambition, you can exercise that now by investing in one young person.

Getting rich and buying your mom a house is a great ambition and a great goal, there are small things you can do to show your mom you appreciate her right now though. Take her out to lunch.

Donating a bunch of sports equipment to an under-resourced community is a wonderful ambition, you could also just purchase a pair of shoes for one athlete that needs help.

You could dream of opening a place for kids to go after school for tutoring someday- that's a wonderful ambition. You could also go the elementary school and ask if you could get matched up with one student that needs some help with his/her homework.

If it is not part of your life right now, even in an infant form, it will not be part of who you are in five years. Money and success just emphasize what is already there.

We don't want to leave on a discouraging note, right? There's good news. You are going to be an emphasized version of who you are now.

You are probably thinking – he just said that.

That's great news because if you are generous, understanding, and invested right now – I can't wait to see the upgrade in five years. What a gift.

CHAPTER 17

The Heartbeat

A couple years ago I almost died. I was on my way to the school I taught at in Detroit, and it was raining. I was driving an F-150 truck. I've always felt comfortable in the rain as a driver. I was about a mile from my exit in the middle lane when I hit a patch of water. My vehicle began to rotate as it planed across the thin layer of water. I did a full rotation before smacking into the center concrete median. It was terrifying and it all went so slow. I hit the median and bounced back into the center of the highway with my passenger side now facing oncoming traffic. A semi-truck was headed right for me. I could tell the driver did his best to avoid me, but it happened so fast, and he rammed right into the front side of my truck. If my car rotated the opposite direction, I wouldn't be here today. My truck came to its final resting place in the grassy hill on the side of the highway. Thankfully I walked away, a little banged up, but I walked away – I was that guy you pass on the highway standing up on the steep hill, looking at his totaled vehicle while people wiz by. It was still raining when the police showed up. They promptly checked both the semi driver and I to make sure we were ok then handed me a ticket for reckless driving. Still a little salty about that to be honest. I went to the hospital to get my head checked out and I was fine, I thought I was fine at least...

A couple weeks later I started having pain in my lower body, it didn't feel good. I remember waking up on a Sunday and I told my wife *I feel like someone kicked me between the legs and it's not going away.* That afternoon we were driving on the highway and my vision started to go, I got really nauseous to the point I had to pull over. I opened the door and fell out of the vehicle, not being able to see and throwing up. *What was wrong with me? This was crazy.*

I went to the emergency room, and they said I looked fine and sent me home. A few days later we welcomed our third child into the world, Amelie. I was there in the hospital room with my wife as she was giving birth, trying to be in the moment while the pain in my lower body increased. I didn't feel like I could say anything about it though, what are you going to say to a woman pushing out a baby? Could someone check me out real quick?

A few days later I woke up and I was in agonizing pain. Without even getting dressed I ran to car and jumped in speeding to the emergency room screaming out loud in pain this time crying and wailing in the car. I was out of my mind in pain. I could barely walk to the front desk of the Emergency Room sobbing trying to tell them about the pain in my lower body. They took me back in a wheelchair, gave me the most painful shot of my life to calm me down, then scanned me all over and could not find the source of the pain. They gave me heavy pain killers and sent me home saying whatever it was would eventually go away.

I took the pain killers daily, but then my left leg began to swell up. *What was wrong with my body?* My leg was twice the size as my other leg. This time I decided to go to a different hospital because the emergency room I was going to could not figure anything out. I drove 30 minutes away this time, parked my car and hobbled into the front desk. I waited there with other people you see in emergency rooms; people hunched over in pain, throwing up in buckets, kids laying in their parents' laps.

They called me back and told me they wanted to do a scan of my leg, a scan of one vein in particular. They put that cold jelly on the scanning device and ran it up and down my left leg. The ultrasound techs can't tell you anything, but I watched her face the whole time and I hated her expression - shock...

"Do you see something?" I asked her.

"Yes." She responded, intentionally holding back. "I do see

something, and you aren't going anywhere for a while."

They moved me to another room in the hospital. A doctor came in and said, "You have no blood flow in your left leg; all the blood has clotted, you will need emergency surgery in the morning."

Emergency surgery, what's going on? Why has the blood stopped flowing in my leg?

In the morning, they took me back for surgery, where they had to remove all the blood from the main vein in my leg because it had all clotted and turned into what appeared to be slugs. It was disgusting and terrifying but they had me on drugs that they usually give to horses, so I was not fully present. I was grateful the surgery was over and just wanted to recover. That night my vitals plummeted, my breathing and my heart rate. I came down with a terrible fever. The doctors were perplexed because I was supposed to stabilize. They scanned my leg again, more clotting further up my leg up near my spine, they had to do the surgery again.

Again.

By this point with the two surgeries, I had been in the hospital for five days and doctors were trying to figure out why my blood was clotting, and why in my leg.

They had determined two things. (1) that I had a genetic mutation my blood called factor five, which means that my blood is more sticky than regular blood. (2) my iliac vein was pinched, which happened as a result of the impact of the car crash.

They informed me that the blood clots had spread to other areas of my body, including one in my lungs. I was scared and it had been a full week in the hospital.

I ended up being able to go home on the 8th day. I have never wanted to hug my kids so bad.

While I was there, I was constantly hooked up to a heart monitor. You look at the screen and see the visual representation of your heartbeat; the straight line, then it takes a sharp climb up, a steep dip down, surfaces back up to the middle and it does it over and

Your life is going to shoot up, it's going to plummet, it's going to normalize and it's going to happen again.

In the medical field when you see a straight line on a heart monitor, it means that person is no longer living.

over again. When you look at the contour of a heartbeat on a monitor you see the rise, fall, and stabilization of the wave form.

This is what it means to be alive, my friends.

Your life is going to shoot up, it's going to plummet, it's going to normalize and it's going to happen again.

In the medical field when you see a straight line on a heart monitor, it means that person is no longer living.

Life whips you around. It's beautiful and it's unfair. It's serene and chaotic. It's dynamic and this is what it means to be alive, it's the heartbeat.

When I look back on the experience, there is a new version of me that emerged from that season. A new version of me with a deeper appreciation for life. A new version of me rethinking my priorities. I had to learn to walk on my leg again with a walker. I had to slow down. I cried on the couch with my wife, and I had never done that before. I was vulnerable and reminded of my own mortality and how fragile I really am no matter how accomplished I may be in life. I'm still just so fragile.

I'm grateful for the hardship and the pain I endured. I remember being in the hospital saying words my therapist told me to reflect on.

"I'm ok, my body is uncomfortable." Indeed, I am ok.

The Monarch

I recently got a tattoo. It's butterfly.

It's my second tattoo - I have wanted tattoos for a long time but just could not settle on something that I would want on my body FOREVER. That's a huge commitment, I better love it, or believe in it or something because it would always be there. Some of my friends have tattoos and they have so much meaning. Some of my other friends have tattoos and they just like to have great art on their bodies. For me, I'd love to meet in the middle. I love relationships and connections so whatever I have on my body, I'd like it to spark a conversation or a connection with someone.

And I was afraid of the pain of a tattoo. I hated that I could not anticipate the pain. I knew what other types of pain felt like - a scratch, a cut, a sprained ankle, or even a broken arm for that matter. I hated I couldn't anticipate the pain of getting a tattoo - But I did it. On our last tour of 2023 the crew and I stopped in a tattoo shop in a little town in Detroit Lakes, MN and I got the word "Faithful" on my forearm in a beautiful cursive script. I had vowed to this specific group nine months prior I was going to do this, and I will always follow through.

It wasn't that bad. My tattoo artist, Matt, was kind and gentle and I tried to zone out looking at all the tattoos on the wall that I would never want on my body!

My first tattoo says "Faithful" because I love this word. I love it. I love to experience faithfulness from others, I love to be faithful, I love to see what happens when you apply it to people and situations. Full of faith, full of belief, resilient, loyal. All of these encompassed in a powerful word that, when put into action can restore and strengthen and bring hope and life when it's applied and made into a commitment. I love it.

So why did I get a butterfly? It's actually more than a butterfly, it's an illusion. You can see the butterfly and its beautiful symmetrical wings but there is an illusion of a skull in the wings. I know, you are probably thinking that's super dark or gothic, but I'd love to explain the meaning to you.

Have you heard of the monarch butterfly? Some kids in elementary get to see them go from caterpillars to butterflies. You come in for school and see your little caterpillar munching on leaves and crawling on sticks inside your little plastic box and a few days later it hangs, encapsuled in a chrysalis it created itself. It hangs there, appearing lifeless as almost its entire body disintegrates away and simultaneously forms a new body with symmetrical beautiful wings that would emerge in a couple weeks. Recreating itself within its own waste. It still is an amazing process to witness - it's a strong dose of awe, that is for sure. It helps you appreciate the incredible balance of the processes that needs to happen just to get that caterpillar to morph into a butterfly. But that is not the reason I got this tattoo on my arm.

Once some of those Monarch butterflies have broken free from their chrysalis, beautiful and vibrant, they fill themselves with milkweed and begin the most astounding migration. Thousands of miles from the Midwest of the United States all the way to Mexico City. An insect. Millions migrating to a place that they have never been or known, yet somehow, they end up in the same place in Mexico. Before they die, they lay eggs, that become caterpillars, that become butterflies, that migrate thousands of miles back north to where their great-great butterfly grandparents were from.

So why the skull illusion in the wings of the Monarch butterfly?

It takes at least four generations of butterflies to make a complete migration. That means once the offspring of the monarchs that originally made it to Mexico start flying back north, it will only be their great-great-great butterfly offspring that will make it back up near Canada.

I have this tattoo for a couple reasons:

1. I want to be part of pushing something meaningful, something worthwhile, beautiful, and valuable forward in my life. Something that maybe my great-great-great grand kids may benefit from.

I want to be part of pushing something meaningful, something worthwhile, beautiful, and valuable forward in my life. Something that maybe my great-great-great grand kids may benefit from.

2. There will be an end to my life, all of our lives actually. The skull has historically held this type of poetic imagery in art. It's not dark or gothic – we all have a skull, actually!

So how about you? I'm obviously not here to endorse tattoos. This is just a decision I wanted to make with my body, and I love that it prompts meaningful conversations with others. Is there an image or piece of art that means something to you? Something that prompts a story or makes you think deep about life and your existence. What did you think of the story I told you today?

PRAY WITH
SOMETHING SAFE
I'm glad
you made
THE LION HEART EXPERIENCE
FOR THE LAST, THE LOST, THE LEAST
AND THE LOOKED OVER
BASED IN DETROIT, MICHIGAN
Thank
being h

RIDE
FOR
FREE
PRIORITY
ELDERLY AND

CHAPTER 19

iPhone on 1%

Has your phone ever been on 1% and you throw it on the charger for an hour, returning to it anticipating at least half of a charge and you discover the charger didn't work, or the outlet didn't work, and your phone is still on 1%, moments from being completely dead? That's the worst, isn't it?

You know some people are like that? You plug into friendship and leave still on 1%. Yikes.

I am not in a place in life where I can have friendships like these.

A few years ago, I sat in my comfy chair in therapy with Jackson, who became one of the champions of my life and he asked me if I could list off any friends I had that I was not mentoring, developing, or leading. I could not even count the people in my life that I genuinely just loved being around without the role of helping to develop, support or shape.

"You need those friendships, Joe." People that you just enjoy being around and they enjoy being around you.

I'm guessing that there's probably a lot of young people reading this book. I almost feel silly telling you this because maybe you've got tons of people around you, classmates, teammates, people by your locker, people on the bus. Yet, most of us (according to research) are so...lonely. On 1% constantly and in need of just a few friendships we can plug into that actually charge us.

I am a public speaker and was in therapy for pervasive depression and anxiety. Still blows me away to sometimes be a living dichotomy. Joe, how do you help young people discover a sense of worth and you feel worthless? It's a constant work.

Can I switch gears for a second? I want to help frame therapy. Do you watch any professional sports? Some of the top performing basketball players like Lebron James or Steph Curry play under a head coach, yes. They also have shooting coaches, nutrition coaches, financial advisors, psychologists, therapists, and athletic trainers to keep their bodies, mind, and skills in top form. They want to be the best.

Now, I'm not aiming to be the best basketball player in the world. But I sure would love to be an amazing husband, I'd like to be a great dad, an awesome public speaker, and last but not least - I would like to enjoy life and love who I am. So, I have coaches for these categories - my wife and I have marriage counselors because if we are in this thing, we want to be good at it and find the best ways to make each other feel alive, supported, and understood. I have a business coach because I want to run a successful business and I need to learn things on how to lead it and make it profitable. I have a therapist because life is hard, and you know just as much as I do that you go through a lot of tough experiences. Experiences that need to be processed with a professional, talked through, learned from, filtered in a healthy way, and filed into our existence.

Having a coach is good.

What areas do you want to excel in? Do you intentionally seek out people to lead you in those areas?

Don't take this as dig, but I do not see this attribute in a lot of young people. In the age of TikTok, YouTube, and Instagram - I see a lot of young people who are amused, and we are super quick to repost an insight we see someone else post.

I always wonder if anyone is actually doing business with the things we repost though. By "do business" I mean spend time with the content, unpack what it means to you and then apply it to your life. Social media can sometimes allow us to play the intellectual part without actually being that person.

Have you ever posted something about mental health, taking care of yourself or loving who you are and felt like a fake because it's not actually how you feel on the inside? You just thought posting it would make you believe it more.

My friend, the most formative experiences and people in your life – you will not find them in a 45-second video. The people that are going to take you into your best-self are waiting for you. In person. You may need to find them.

Look for the people ahead of you in life, in love, in skill, in money, in networks. Find them and ask them to coach you.

Who makes you feel recharged?

CHAPTER 20

Donuts

When I was in 4th grade I loved to bake. I would make all types of cookies and pies and cakes. Before Snapchat streaks I had my own streak going of bringing something to my teacher, Ms. Phillips every day for 30 days straight.

I remember being so confident in my baking abilities I asked if my dad could go to his corporate tech job and take orders on an excel sheet. I always had a little bit of hustle in me. Nothing was professional grade, but I was not bad as a little 10-year-old baker. I had a dream that I might own a bakery someday. We had a local shop called Hamilton's that served the best donuts. I can still smell the shop in my memory, walking in and smelling sugar in the air, looking behind the curved glass to see all types of donuts and believing I could eat every single one. The chocolate milk from the little fridge they had in the corner tasted so good even though it was probably the same chocolate milk I got at school.

One night at around 3:00 AM my dad woke me up. "Joe, Joe" he whispered softly so he wouldn't wake up my little brother sleeping above me in our bunk beads.

"Joe, get dressed I want to take you somewhere."

I got dressed in my clothes and slipped on my shoes. We stepped outside into the mix of night and morning; it was mid-fall so I could see my breath while we walked to our minivan crunching leaves beneath our feet.

It was a workday for my dad; I knew he would have to be into his job around 8:00 AM and I had school. I sat in the front seat waiting for the heater in the car to start kicking out some warmth.

"We are going somewhere special buddy," my dad said warmly to me.

After a familiar 15-minute ride to the small downtown of where I live, we pulled into Hamilton's. I could see bright lights illuminating the inside back of the business, not lights on in the front though. No customers. No one walking around outside.

We walked up to the front door and a lady let us in the front door, carefully unlocking it from the inside. There was a bell attached to the door that would jingle when it shut. I can still hear it.

My dad and I walked behind the counter and through a single door into a bright kitchen. Bags of flour sat on the floor, mixing bowls and mixers stood firmly on the counter, pots and pans hung above our heads, and men in white aprons moved around the kitchen.

"You must be Joey," one of the bakers said to me, extending his hand out to greet me. "Your dad says you might want to be a baker someday and asked if you might be able to come in and see how the magic happens." He continued, "We were thinking maybe you could help us get some of our classics mixed up and ready for the day." I eagerly agreed, now fully awake both in my mind and body, excited to learn and participate with guys who actually make donuts.

I spent the next 3-4 hours mixing and pouring, flipping donuts in oil, and learning to create twists, dipping them in icing and getting the jellies and cremes inside the pastries. I felt so real, so alive, like a legit baker. The whole morning for me went by so fast and at the end, the bakers let me take an entire box with me to give to my class that morning in school.

This is a vivid memory for me. It was an identity moment that my dad facilitated; he was really good at those – still is.

My dad could have given me a pat on the back, biting into a cookie I made when he would get home from work. Instead, he calls up the local bakery and asks if he can bring in his 10-year-old to help make donuts at 3:00 AM on a day he also has to go to work for 8 hours. He decided to enter into my world, to be on my level, and offer me a small taste of what my dreams could become.

I didn't grow up to own a bakery. Although, like most people, I will never pass up a donut.

But inside of myself I carry a memory. It's warm and covered in flour, it tastes like sugar and crème. It feels like putting on an apron to operate in a world that you know you are not big enough or qualified enough to work in. It sounds like sizzling oil and industrial mixers... This memory helps me as a dad myself, now with three young children. It moves me to always make time to enter into the little worlds and dreams of my kids and to try my best to offer them the same types of experiences.

> I didn't grow up to own a bakery... But inside of myself I carry a memory. It's warm and covered in flour, it tastes like sugar and crème.

Grande Three-Shot Two-Pump, Cinnamon Dulce Latte

I love to learn little things about people. I frequently take notes in my phone when I hear people in my circle say things I would like to remember. My wife, Heather loves a grande three-shot two-pump cinnamon dulce latte from Starbucks. My business coach, Rick, loves a grande, decaf, cappuccino with coconut milk. When we are on tour, I know Tae loves the gummy Life Savers from the gas station. Jeremiah, our sound engineer, enjoys the peach Red Bull when he's driving and if he is tired, he will buy an Excedrin for the caffeine boost.

I like to take notes of little things that people enjoy so I can bless them with something personalized that they like. I even remember stories I like to keep tucked away. Like Julie, one of our singers – she was in Mexico and rode a horse that was later featured in a group meal! Wild. Our stories, the things we delight in, our favorites, they are the fabric of who we are.

> I like to take notes of little things that people enjoy so I can bless them with something personalized that they like.

Memories build people.

When I run in the gas station on a short stop on the road and throw a package of Life Saver gummies to Tae (who is usually sleeping). It's a little way of letting him know I am paying attention to big things and little things about him.

It feels good to be known. To be thought of. Tae does the same thing for me – he will grab me an Arnold Palmer and some barbeque chips. So good on the road.

Sometimes Jeremiah will put his hand on my shoulder and give me a specific compliment, "I like how you used the space and your dynamic range in the performance today, good job." He knows I appreciate specific positive feedback.

Being known feels like belonging and every single person is looking for that. Start taking some notes.

Mayonnaise

I do not like mayonnaise (mayo). When we are on tour, if a school gets us sandwiches for lunch and they come with mayo - I am almost unable to touch the sandwich. I'm not even that high maintenance of a person. I just can't do it. I need to distance myself from mayo. Both flavor and texture are the inhibitors for me. I can't scrape it off or just remove parts of the sandwich it touches. Mayonnaise is that bad.

Despite the terribleness and personal aversion to mayo - I find it undeniably intriguing. I am most interested because the two main ingredients in mayo are oil and water. If you've ever seen oil and water in a container, they immediately separate. The oil floats on top because it is less dense than water, the two liquids are immiscible - they can't mix or dissolve into each other. On a molecular level - in precise scientific language - they cannot stand each other.

Their molecules will not allow it! Even if you vigorously shake a bottle of water and oil, it will inevitably separate.

Except in mayo. The two main ingredients are oil and water, yet mayo is never separating in a jar. It's the same terrible, off-white, creamy, awful texture all the time. All the time! Why?

Mayonnaise has something in it called an emulsifier - egg. An emulsifier is a compound that allows things like water and oil to mix, bond, and exist together in the same mixture. I know, there's egg in mayonnaise! I can't! In a metaphorical way, egg stands in between water and oil with a hand extended to both saying, "trust me."

Yet, I am inextricably drawn to the concept of mayo with my brain, not with my tastebuds. An emulsifier keeps things that would otherwise separate, ingredients that would naturally dissent from each other - together.

Now to my final point and leading challenge when I look at mayonnaise.

I want to be an egg. Despite its insidious use on sandwiches - mayonnaise stands as an open challenge to all of us sandwich consumers. That two very different substances can exist together, bonded.

What might this challenge us in today? For me, as silly as it sounds, I want to be an egg. #Lifegoals.

I want to be an emulsifier in life. Through learning and developing skills inside of myself like Compassion, understanding, patience, and belief - I can operate in life, family, schools, and inside The Lion Heart crew with hands extended to groups, people, and situations that would never fuse together. Being an emulsifier means you can transcend boundaries and barriers - doesn't that sound amazing?

> Being an emulsifier means you can transcend boundaries and barriers — doesn't that sound amazing?

Do you know any eggs in your life? Go tell them about mayonnaise, let them know they've inspired you today.

CHAPTER 23

The Dad Bod

Shoot. I dated a cheerleader in college. I cared nothing for football at the University we both attended but if I was going to go to the games – you better believe I'm going to be one of those guys with my chest painted in the middle of November in the front row because the girl I'm falling for is down there near the endzone. I have to be close with some deep digging online you might find these pictures.

I didn't look too bad out there, honestly! I was pretty in-shape. Something worked out anyway because I ended up marrying that cheerleader.

My last couple years of college I would get up early with some of my friends and go lift weights early in the morning. College is when I probably felt the best about my body and how I looked. I continued exercising after leaving college and starting as a teacher in Detroit. I would get up early with a roommate and go to LA Fitness half-asleep to lift things, talk about life, sit in the sauna and shower before heading to school. My eating was even really simple - I would eat a pre-packaged bag of Caesar salad and a chicken breast most nights.

That was ten years ago – now I am ten years into marriage and three kids deep. My wife and I still work out regularly, but things are a little different. Ten years changes your metabolism, kids shift your eating, having a spouse shifts how you eat. I can tell you with 100% certainty, I have arrived at the dad bod. Nothing over the top but a little puffy. The guys I travel with in Lion Heart are so fit, sometimes I feel self-conscious about my own fitness. I'm trying out here fam!

I have learned this about fitness though - and it will benefit you. Physical fitness is one of the many realms of fitness.

> Physical fitness is one of the many realms of fitness. I know some people who are physically fit, they look amazing — and they are terrible people.

I know some people who are physically fit, they look amazing - and they are terrible people. They are unaware of anyone else's experience around them and lack a huge amount of empathy and understanding. I have some friends who are super in shape and drowning in financial debt. That's not fitness. I have some friends who have amazing bodies and struggle to maintain healthy friendships and can't commit in a relationship. That's not fitness. I've got some friends layered with muscle and tone who don't ever read a book, pursue healthy habits, or really learn much of anything. That's not fitness. I've got friends who are skinny and toned and an emotional wreck, burdened by unresolved trauma and lack of emotional intelligence. That is not fitness. To be fit is to pursue health in all areas.

Fitness should benefit the people close to you.

Maybe I'm just trying to feel better about the 20 lbs. I need to lose. Or maybe I'm on to something - you can be the judge.

If you want to be fit, could I challenge you in a few ways? Write down the areas of your life where fitness exists. You might consider writing down some categories like physical, mental, emotional, relational, and financial and track what you do each day to move toward fitness in those categories. I do this actually; I have a daily tracker where I either plan my day or reflect on my day and make sure I am doing something in all of these categories. I may be rocking the dad bod for a second here but I am really grateful to have cultivated a wonderful marriage with that cheerleader. My favorite times with Heather are staying up late on the couch to talk and ordering Taco Bell at 11 p.m. It's not healthy but you know what - it also feeds into the relational fitness of my connection with my wife. How do you see fitness?

The Most Important Intersection

How do I find my place in the world? What am I meant to do? Who am I meant to be?

Big questions, right? The biggest and most important questions, actually.

Some people spend their whole lives trying to figure this out or leading others to a realization of a true sense of self and purpose. If your heart is open, I'd love to offer you a reflection as you are on this journey.

When I was young, I attended a retreat where I heard a speaker get up in front of a room of college students to talk on a life worth living. I zoned out for most of the talk until he said, "Do you want to know who you are meant to be, where you are meant to go, what you were born to do?"

Yes, I do want to know that. Don't we all, I looked around the room feeling like I'm the only person who woke up for a moment. Can this guy help me figure that out?

"Your place in the world..." he said slowly as I began to scratch his words down onto a scrap piece of paper. "Your place in the world is at the intersection of your deepest passions, where you feel the most alive and the world's deepest need. It's only in this place where you will find the deepest contentment, joy, fulfillment, purpose, and endurance to carry on."

The intersection of my deepest passion and the world's greatest needs.

Over the next couple years of college, I pursued my degree in music education. This mentality led me to my first school where the interview committee for the music teacher position in this inner-city Detroit school said, "Our kids come from tough backgrounds, not a lot of fathers in the home, not a lot of stability." Offering the acceptance of a father, the unflinching belief of a father is who I am. I have always been this person. Maybe it's because I'm the oldest of 7 kids but offering my affirmation, love, and delight is who I have always been. Was this job made for me?

"We have no instruments here."

No problem, I had spent the last five years traveling to street corners all around the United States with just a guitar and had to create meaningful moments with no resources. I was made for this job.

It was at this school that I met Tae, now the premier Lion Heart touring artist with our group. He was a fifth grader, and I was a first-year teacher figuring out life. Somehow, a long time ago - our lives were meant to intersect at this school to begin what would later become The Lion Heart Experience.

Your adventure, your greatest life rests at this intersection — young person.

At the intersection of two points, the place where your greatest passion meets the world's deepest need.

Your adventure, your greatest life rests at this intersection - young person.

At the intersection of two points, the place where your greatest passion meets the world's deepest need.

I hope to meet this version of you someday.

CHAPTER 25

I'm Sorry, Will You Accept My Apology?

In The Lion Heart Crew, our apologies take a long time. We spend a lot of time together so there's a ton of potential to step on each other's toes, annoy someone, or screw up an unspoken expectation. When we do - it's best to take responsibility for it. So, we apologize, but not in the way you may have experienced. We do something that we call an "all the way apology." It looks like this. I'll use an example with Jeremiah because I sometimes say harsh or passive-aggressive things when I'm under a lot of pressure:

"Jeremiah, I am sorry that I _____________ (say what I did), it must have made you feel _______________ (say how I believe it made him feel). I don't want you to ever feel that way. Will you please forgive me? (wait and let him respond). Is there anything else you would like me to know or that I may have missed?"

That's a lot more than we learned in kindergarten, isn't it? Most of us still apologize the same way we did in grade school, "I'm sorry, will you accept my apology?" Or even shorter, just, "I'm sorry."

Here's the problem with that. An apology without acknowledging the

> An apology without acknowledging the impact of what you did — is not an apology and the beauty of a sincere apology opens the door for something beautiful called "repair."

impact of what you did – is not an apology and the beauty of a sincere apology opens the door for something beautiful called "repair."

If you really care about a relationship and you messed up – look at that person, put your hand on their shoulder, look in their eyes and follow our approach to apologies. You will see a real increase in the health of your relationships.

1. Admit what you did. "I am so sorry that I was passive aggressive with you."

2. Say how you believe it made them feel. "That must have made you feel disrespected and confused, that's not fair to you."

3. Ask them to forgive you. "Will you forgive me for that?"

4. Ask them if there is anything else they would like you to know, understand or if there is anything else you had missed.

The most successful relational connections embrace the concept of repair[10] and pay close attention to the areas of their life that it is needed.

What if they don't forgive you?

Then they don't forgive you. The all the way apology is for *your* health. Do it the right way and watch your friends respect you more and start to believe that you genuinely care about the relationship.

CHAPTER 26

Anti-Bullying

"I think I may have misrepresented who you guys were to our principals," the woman said who contracted us to come and present in front of their high school students.

"I thought you guys were an anti-bullying assembly."

We get this a lot actually. It's October and that is apparently the month set aside to address bullying, so schools and counselors and presenters like us take their best shot at stopping bullying in schools.

Here's my thing though. Once you say, "we're going to talk about bullying," students check out. Am I wrong? Let me build out my reasoning and cast a vision for something else.

Bullying is so layered and disguised and veiled now. Especially with phones. I don't even like the term "cyber-bullying" because it still prompts some type of cartoon-like image in our minds of a big bully attacking a smaller, weaker student.

No. Bullying at its core is chipping away at someone's self-worth, identity, and value. Through looks and words and glances and texts, and the way you use your body – you chip away at the value of another person. If you have been to a Lion Heart performance, you may remember the canvas. Bullying means you are creating a mess. On a canvas where that person would love to see something beautiful come together for their life you dip a brush and fling the paint onto the canvas; you smear and deface anything that looks like it could be something.

> Bullying is all about worth — and that is what Lion Heart is about. That is the core issue of bullying, you are attacking someone's worth.

Bullying is all about worth – and that is what Lion Heart is about. That is the core issue of bullying, you are attacking someone's worth. You can do it with a phone, you can do it by the way you intentionally exclude someone, you can do it through a passive aggressive text or look in the hallway.

Here's my other issue with anti-bullying. Let's say you do the impossible and rid your school of bullying. Have you built something meaningful? Or have you just gotten rid of something bad? I am so much more concerned with what a school is building, what students are building, what staff are building than what they are trying to remove.

When I am in a school, my goal is to sell my audience on the idea that you could paint something beautiful today with your words, with your presence, by the way you go out of your way to sit next to someone or let them know you are glad they made it.

I want to make a hard pivot here. When my kids were born and as they grew, I was increasingly aware of their ability to make a mess and destroy things. I'd build a tower of blocks with my infant son, Eli, and he would knock it down. I'd clean the house and he would make a mess and leave it. We would be drawing with crayons, and he'd be more interested in scribbling on my picture than creating his own. Can you believe how irresponsible 1-year olds are? This is where I'm going with this. Somehow, we are born with the innate ability to make a mess and tear something down. It comes naturally to us as illustrated by any baby. I had to teach Eli to build a tower, I had to teach him to clean up his mess, I had to teach him to draw. We must be taught to make beautiful things with effort, or we will default into our hidden infant selves, now disguised on our Instagram profile or in a football jersey and revert back to our natural draw to destroy and make a mess.

This is why our program is the perfect anti-bullying presentation.

Because we are focused on helping schools build something great. Encouraging students and staff to uphold the value of each other in their words and actions. Not to chip away at the value of others but to push against that natural urge to knock down someone else's tower instead of help them build it. Or to beautify a space instead of mess it up. To look at a blank canvas or a person and think "how can I help something magical happen here?"

How can you make magic happen today?

Are you chipping away or adding to others today? Why?

But What If I Die?

A few years ago, I was in the hospital for some serious blood clots in my leg. I have a blood condition called Factor Five Liden which basically means that my blood is more sticky than regular people's blood. That combined with a vein in my lower back called The Iliac vein that is supposed to run parallel with another but instead crosses over sometimes put me at risk for developing blood clots that can be deadly.

After my first experience with blood clots and an 8 day stay in the hospital I was sent home with some chilling news - blood clots that had developed in my leg had traveled through my bloodstream up near my lungs. There wasn't much they could do besides inform me, put me on blood-thinners and hope for the best.

The following nights I would lay in bed afraid to move, afraid wondering if the blood clots might dislodge, move to my heart or my brain and I would die. I would lay awake in bed hoping that the position of my body would not lend itself to the movement of the blood clots close to my vitals.

In a session with my Therapist, Jackson, I opened up to him about these fears that kept me up, stole my sleep and my energy.

"It's hard sleeping knowing something so close to killing me is inches away from my lungs and my heart. What if I die? That's what

I'm thinking when I'm trying to sleep."

"That makes sense," Jackson said to me looking over his tortoise framed glasses. He scribbled a note on his note pad.

"You need to balance those thoughts though, yea?" He continued. "Those are pretty natural *what if* thoughts, what if the worst thing happens. Try balancing them with the opposite *what if's*, out loud." He continued, guiding me as I watched him speak them out loud to demonstrate how I could do this.

"What if I sleep the best I've ever slept tonight"

"What if my body works on my behalf to wear down the blood-clot to reabsorb it into my blood stream."

"What if tomorrow I am actually more healthy, balanced and rested than I was today."

This session with Jackson was a powerful practice and reminder to me to balance my what if's. Perhaps it may help you as well in your worries. Maybe you are worried about something going on with your body, a sickness – your mind is flooded with *what if this beats me* thoughts. You are taking a job and you are suffering emotionally burdening yourself with *what if I'm not qualified enough to do this* thoughts. Maybe you are in a relationship and you can't help it but allow the insecurities and hurts from the past saturate your thoughts, *what if she leaves, what if he leaves, what if I'm hurt again and look stupid.*

If I could share Jackson, my Therapist, with you. You can imagine him sitting in his therapist chair, looking at you over the rims of his brown tortoise glasses. He's got tattoos and jogger-style dress pants on. He's tall but always sitting, clean-shaven with strawberry blonde short hair combed stylishly to the side.

"Let's balance out those worried thoughts, Friend" I would imagine him saying to you, my friend that I've brought to my session today. Jackson want's to see you alive and full of hope, I do too.

What if your body, that balances all types of delicate processes without your guidance – what if it works on your behalf tonight while you sleep.

What if this job that worries you turns out to be a perfect fit, bringing about the most amazing growth and relationships.

What if this relationship is not like the others and all the good you have put into the world may be coming back to you.

Give it a shot. I'm with you.

CHAPTER 28

RJ

I had a bully in 4th grade. His name was RJ. I feel like I can use his name, seems to be working for Taylor Swift haha. It was a classic bullying scenario too, not as nuanced and layered as it is today. What felt like every day in Ms. Philips class, RJ would use his body to block my path to my seat or use his shoulder to shove me as I walked past. He was a little goofy guy too. Probably one of the smallest people in the class and even smaller than me. I have a vivid memory of him pressing his finger into an empty box that had previously contained light bulbs for science experiments with electricity currents. Some of the light bulbs had broken and he pressed his finger into the box to intentionally cut his index finger causing it to bleed and lick the blood of his finger to get nervous, but affirming, laughs of my classmates.

I felt embarrassed whenever RJ would push me. Often because it would come with some type of name calling, insult, or at least a couple laughs of students nearby.

I was confused too. I grew up in the church and all I could think was "turn the other cheek" from Sunday school class. Or that maybe I should pray for him or let it go or tell him, "I forgive you" when he would harass me.

I went home one night and brought it up to my parents at dinner.

"Joe, next time that happens I want you to shove him down as hard as you can," my dad said.

That was even more confusing to me. You want me to shove him? With my dad starting a job at the church, I was surprised that was the wisest advice he could give.

The next day, the same thing happened. I could see RJ ready to block my path to my seat and I tried to move past him. He moved to body check me with his shoulder. I lifted my hands up to place them on his chest and pushed as hard as I could, "leave me alone!" I shouted as he fell to the ground. What happened after that is a little blurry, I just remember almost being sick it felt so out of character for me. I know we both had to leave the class and sit in the principal's office for some reason.

You can't teach a kid to turn a cheek he doesn't have. I am a naturally understanding and forgiving person. Kids like me are sometimes not only mistaken for being weak, but we actually are also. We can become targets because we are nice people, and it takes having to push back and raise your voice to realize you are more than that. I am more than nice.

> You can't teach a kid to turn a cheek he doesn't have.

Play with something safe, I told em' never play with me.
-Tae Sosa

CHAPTER 29

Predicting the Weather

How are you feeling about the weather these days? I'm curious what season it is as you read this. As you look outside, what natural processes to you see happening?

Is rain falling from the sky? Millions of pounds of water that somehow end up stored in clouds that form from the evaporation of water on the earth back up into the atmosphere... Is it returning to the ground?

Is the sun shining today? The sun that, no matter what is happening in my life, seems to rise and set each day on both my victories and my troubles. It rises and sets on my deepest joys and loneliest tears. The sun that, if we were any closer to it, would make our planet uninhabitable due to the burning temperatures it would heat our surface to. Or if we were further away, would create a much different life in sub-zero Antarctic conditions. What an incredible balance we live in just with the sun.

Are leaves blooming or falling today? Where I'm writing this right now, from my home office in Detroit, the last bit of leaves are starting to fall off the trees. The most brilliant oranges and reds and yellows have turned to different shades of brown; the snow will be here soon. The trees will look dead – yet somehow in the spring, tiny buds will appear just like they did last year, and these trees will bloom with flowers and then rich green leaves.

Are you near water? A large lake or ocean? Does the water move? Do the waves crash themselves against the shore without being told to do that or does the tide bring the water closer, then pull it back depending on the time of day. Amazing.

Have you got your vitamin D today? I used to think that vitamin D came from the sun. That was one of the only things I remember from science class. I was wrong! All this time. I learned that it's actually my body that creates vitamin D, within the cells in my blood that I can't see but are constantly working on behalf of my health. When I step into the sun, my body is triggered and begins to produce the vitamin D I need to be healthy and balanced. The sun's rays just start the process.

So many delicate natural processes around me and inside of me. It always gives me a small dose of awe. It helps me gain perspective on my life as well – that no matter what happens to me, which could seem huge or devastating. *I am a small piece in a big, big universe.* I love this quote from the character, Hushpuppy, in the movie "Beasts of the Southern Wild."

"When it all goes quiet behind my eyes, I see everything that made me lying around in invisible pieces. When I look too hard, it goes away. And when it all goes quiet, I see they are right here. I see that I'm a little piece in a big, big universe. And that makes things right…"

Let's get back to the weather. What do you expect will happen today with the temperature or precipitation? I like to watch the meteorologists predict the weather on TV. Somehow like trying to anticipate the attitude and actions of a friend, they stand in front of that camera and tell me where the winds will be coming from. If a cold front is moving in, whether I will see clouds today or if rain may fall from the sky. They slow down, speed up, and freeze, the upcoming cloud movements and intensities of precipitation. They predict the movement of storms and hurricanes and where they will touch land as they form over the ocean. They know the weather; they can't change the weather but they are skilled enough to know it and predict it.

Do you know where I am going with this?

You are part of nature. We talked about this before. I often can find myself thinking that I just operate within nature, or nature is around me to be appreciated, worked with, considered, protected, and worked around.

But I am nature as well.

All those amazing, fragile processes I talked about up earlier with the clouds and leaves, tides and seasons. In some way all of those are reflected inside of me as well. All of them.

Thoughts, emotions, experiences, words, fears all accumulate inside of me like a cloud – at some point there is going to be a release that happens. Prompted by me or not, these thoughts, emotions, experiences, words, and fears will be expressed. Just as the rain cannot stay hidden, so it is with the world that happens on the inside.

Are you in a season of feeling alive? Bursting with life and color like the trees in the spring? Or are you in a season of feeling lifeless, slow, shallow, and alone? If I can accept the seasons that happen around me can I also accept the seasons that happen inside of me.

Are the waves coming in and out during your day, do you sense times when you need to rest and pull back and times you are eager and inspired? Do you know yourself in that way to anticipate the waves and rhythms of your life? What would life be like if we were to understand the waves, currents, and tides inside of us?

I'm trying to lead you into an understanding of a word called self-compassion. It's the ability to understand yourself to a point that can give yourself grace, space, time, and forgiveness. It's having an understanding of yourself that informs your activities and friend groups. Self-compassion is learning, that as you should be a friend to others that you must also be a friend to yourself.

The title of this book was going to be, "it might not be ok, but you could be." No matter how hard you try, you will not change the processes already happening in nature. You will not stop the rain or the tide. You will not stop the processes happening in that tree unless you chop it down. Still then you have not stopped nature - you just removed one expression.

I cannot predict the weather that will happen in your life, what emotional experiences await you. What cold and warm fronts will move in during your high school years or where the winds will come from while you are a young adult. I cannot predict how long seasons of growth and love and seasons of loneliness and sadness will last - but they will come.

You are part of nature.

Now, there is amazing news within all of this. You cannot change the weather, but you can know yourself well enough - just as a meteorologist knows the weather like a friend - there is a way to try to anticipate and respond to seasons on a macro and micro level so that you can keep a beautiful perspective on your life and experience.

Can I speak to you from personal experience? Just yesterday I woke up and did what I usually do, I had coffee and read on the couch. I got my kids ready for school and dropped them off. I went to the gym and got my mile run in and some lifting. I returned home to get some work done. Each day I try to make sure I build something in for my heart (my quiet coffee time or a good conversation with my wife), my mind (reading/learning/listening to a podcast), my strength (a workout or pursuing a goal) and my soul (meditation, prayer, asking for forgiveness). I pay attention to these four categories because I have learned that if I do pay attention to them, I have the best chance at a great day.

I returned from the gym and got some work done. I sat at my computer and was overwhelmed with heaviness and discouragement. Don't ask me why, but it happened. The weather changed and I tried for about an hour to push through it and grind it out. I ended up with my head down on my desk. A cold front had moved in. Now, because I am working on self-compassion and understanding I tried to embrace the idea that weather in my life is dynamic, it's always shifting. I can do what I can to try and work within it - and sometimes I need to yield to the weather. So, I went to the couch to lay down, I set my alarm for 27 minutes and dozed off. My alarm went and off and I set it again for another 27 minutes. It was then time to go pick up my kids, put dinner together, and do the bedtime routine with my kids. All of this happened while I was still feeling heavy and discouraged.

Today I woke up rested, I had a great idea while I was sitting on the couch having coffee and my kids were making a slushy by crushing up ice and mixing it with Pepsi in the kitchen at 8:00 AM. I am sitting here writing and I feel encouraged and inspired, I feel balanced and regulated. I'm grateful for the words that have come to mind today when nothing happened yesterday. I feel good today and I'm taking advantage of it.

We are in a culture that is going to tell you to push through and grind no matter what you are feeling. Like a football player in the middle of a game, it doesn't matter how you feel, get out there and win.

This is not that type of book. I'm not endorsing a lifestyle where you just go take a nap when there's something you don't want to do, either. What I am trying to help you understand, dear young person, is that it is a beautiful and meaningful thing to know yourself. You cannot love yourself any more than you know yourself and to get to know the seasons, processes, and patterns that exist within you is a wonderful thing. I'm on the road with you.

I'm a Leader

I used to use a saying to bring my class together in my inner-city Detroit classroom. It was catchy and fun and loud. It sounded like this:

Me: I'm the head
Students: not the tail
Me: I'm above
Students: Not Beneath
Me: I'm a leader
Students: Not a follower

For years I used this chant. After the students would vigorously shout it back at me, that would be our cue to begin class –
focus in – and start our day with a jolt of energy and positivity. I especially loved this chant because I taught in an area with a lot of disenfranchised and marginalized people groups. My whole class was Black and/or Latino.

Side note, when I first started teaching – I was the only light-skinned person in the room. I was the only milk. I was the only vanilla, and man was I vanilla. I had some learning to do. More on that later. Back to this chant.

I loved this chant because it was position and perspective shifting. I wanted my students to internalize, even if it was from this silly chant,

that they deserved to be in places of influence and power and that
their voices deserved to be heard and recognized in all circles. I still
believe that.

I started running into a problem though. Basically, right away.
Right after I would shout the last part "I'm a leader" and the kids
would shout "not a follower" - they would do just that. Not follow
directions, or instructions, or expectations.

Dang. I made my own loophole.

In fact, I did want them to follow. I wanted them to follow....me.
To participate in what I had planned for our learning for the day.
I wanted them to catch the artistic vision of the music we would
create and follow me. The problem was that I just had them
shout back with all their might and angst "I'm a leader - NOT A
FOLLOWER".

Later I would learn that this simple phrase is reinforcing something
that we deal with constantly in our world. It's called polarizing.

That means we only offer two options and they are always extreme.
Here's some examples:
You're in or you are out.
You are with me or against me.
There are only two types of people in this world
Or...
You're either a leader or a follower.

Leader being good. Follower being bad.

This is called polarizing, and it's not good for a couple different
reasons: I'll get to those in a second. Let's hang out on this Leader/
Follower theme for a second.

I've got two amazing teammates in The Lion Heart Experience. Tae,
who's songs/stories/insights and presence make The Lion Heart
Experience memorable and impactful for students all around the
country. I've also got Jeremiah, our sound engineer, who does
the bulk of our driving. He manages all our sound equipment and
builds all the Lion Heart frames. Here's the thing. I am grateful that
they allow me to lead. I'm grateful that they trust me and listen to

my direction for The Lion Heart Experience. I'm grateful that they bring the best of their gifts and talents to a worthwhile mission and vision. I'm grateful that they follow.

In a talk I give for high school seniors called, "What to do with your life when you don't know what to do with your life." I tell young people that if you have no idea what to do – get behind someone who knows exactly what they are doing and where they are going. Get behind someone with vision and mission and purpose and...follow. Not in a way that we follow on social media, I mean you bring the best of yourself. I mean that you go to them, tell them you want to be part of the dream, offer the gifts and skills you have to push the dream forward. Follow.

In this talk I let young people know that if you do this for a couple years and it has not led you closer to your next step in life... If following a great person does not bring you closer to a sense of purpose... If supporting a beautiful dream and vision of a great leader does not leave you more full of life than you were two years ago – I'll take you out to dinner wherever you'd like and let you tell me to my face, "You were wrong." You can even order dessert.

Here's the thing, we all need to know how to follow well AND the world needs followers. Some of the most wonderful people that have made the biggest impact on me in my life are helpers. People who can anticipate needs, step into gaps and you can trust them completely, people you can assign something to and they say, "No problem, I'm on it." Those people inspire me.

> Here's the thing, we all need to know how to follow well AND the world needs followers. Some of the most wonderful people that have made the biggest impact on me in my life are helpers.

I'm trying to deconstruct our understanding of a follower – or at least try to disconnect it from a negative association. Of course, I believe things like this as well, "Bad company corrupts good character," or "Show me your friends and I'll show you your future." They are a little oversimplified, but the principles are solid.

Life is nuanced. There's a keyword for you, circle it and look it up so you can use it. That means life not usually simple. It's layered and complicated by multiple perspectives and understandings.

Doing the right thing can often leave you feeling really bad. People who tell you the truth and love you can often make you feel like they could be against you. Your stance on an issue that's hot and controversial in the news like immigration, gay marriage, abortion – they all may shift when that issue actually becomes a person sitting across from you. When you listen to their stories and experiences, something shifts. Life is nuanced. It's layered and it's complicated. It's not as simple as being a leader or a follower. It's not as simple as being in or out. With us or against us.

I'd argue that the most differentiated and successful people are both leaders and followers – that's my goal at least. I would love to lead my family well. I aspire to lead The Lion Heart Experience well – my hope is that people who work within our organization feel a real sense of transformation, purpose, and genuine care from me. I also desire to follow well, to support well, to ride next to amazing people and support their dreams with the best of my time and talents and resources. I want to follow well; I want to sit under the teaching and coaching of the people I aspire to be like.

...

Polarizing is a great thing to call out when you see it. If you are looking to sharpen your skills – try watching the news. That's a great place to practice. See how often headlines and stories cast only two types of people (i.e. democrats vs. republicans) only two extreme stances on an issue (i.e. pro-life or pro-choice). Watch interviews where the two people push to make the gap between them as large as possible when, in reality, they actually agree on most things.

Polarizing is dangerous because it takes us away from the reality that most of us really do want the same things.

Be a leader and a follower.

CHAPTER 31

Two Quarters

When I was a kid, I had some heros. I was like most kids and collected sports cards and posters of NBA, NFL, and MLB players. Little Caesar's Pizza used to give away 6-foot posters of football players with specific pizzas. I loved to collect them I would put them up on my wall not even caring who they were. I thought it was cool to have sports stars in my room. I had not yet discovered 100% that I was not very good at football, basketball, or baseball. That would come later.

There were a few people I thought the world of that weren't featured on a card or a poster. Any time we were in a big city I'd get to see these people. Actually, I'd hear them before I would see them. Street musicians.

People who could create the most insane beats with a bucket and some pots and pans. Dancers would do crazy stunts jumping over audience members or show impressive balance, magicians who could draw in a crowd with mystifying tricks. Guitar players, singers, saxophone players: they all intrigued me so much. Putting a dollar in their case or their hat or their bucket never seemed like enough to me. These were the most confident people I could imagine. Putting their skills out there for the world to react to as they see fit. Some would stop to watch, others completely ignored them, some pulled out their cameras to record, people sat interested, some walked past annoyed.

Street musicians were my heroes. I would think to myself *my dream is to be as confident as they are doing what they do.* It was their incredible crowd skills and musicianship that I looked up to, but it was also their sheer (perceived) confidence.

> Street musicians were my heroes. I would think to myself my dream is to be as confident as they are doing what they do.

I wanted that.

I would continue to grow through elementary school. I did eventually discover that my lack of that killer-instinct would keep me from having what it took to be dominant on the football field, basketball court, or wrestling mat. In baseball I was terrified that the pitcher would be aiming that ball right at my rib cage. I started taking guitar lessons in 5th grade, I pretty much hated it right away because of the learning curve. With guitar, you sound bad for a long time before you sound good. Your fingers hurt, they don't move the way you want them to, or as fast as you want them to. I wanted to quit, and my parents didn't let me, they made me practice because they said, "you wanted to do this, you stick with it."

Eventually I didn't suck. I was not bad. Around 8th grade I took some great strides with my guitar playing and could keep up pretty well on the instrument. I still didn't sing though, no way would I sing. I knew I could, but man, if I sang and people laughed at me – I wasn't sure if I could take it. This is middle school, it's rough out here!

High school was right around the corner, and I had a realization. I was going to have a chance to go to 9th grade in a new building, with new people, and new teachers who didn't know who I was.

If there's a chance to reinvent yourself, I knew now was the time. My mind reflected back on my childhood and how much I still looked up to street performers with their courage and skill. I hadn't yet found my thing. Even with guitar, no one really likes to watch you just strum the guitar...you gotta sing.

I learned to sing and play one song that I thought sounded ok and one night decided I was going to not live scared. I took my guitar downtown and stood kiddy corner to the corner I knew was where

I should take a stab at street performing. Kiddy corner means, the other side of the street.

I hadn't tried street performing before, but all I knew was if I sucked – I did not want to be on the busiest corner in my hometown. So, there I was across the street. I sat down with my guitar and folded up my case and put it behind me. I took a breath and started singing.

"Cause it's you and me, and all other people, with nothing to do, nothing to lose." I was taking a solid swing at this sappy Lifehouse song that was popular at the time.

"Cause it's you and me and all other people and I don't know why, I can't keep my eyes off of you."

I glanced up to see a woman standing about 7 feet in front of me listening. I only knew one song so when I finished, I just said "hi." It was so awkward – what else was I going to do? Play the same song again. She reached into her pocket and pulled out two quarters and set them at my feet.

"Hi," she said. "You're pretty good, why don't you have your guitar case open?"

I blurted out some blatant teenage insecurity response. Something confident but 100% untrue and said "oh, I forgot" knowing full well that I didn't have it out because I was thinking no one would drop money in it, I was sure of it.

She left the two quarters stacked on top of each other right in front of me and walked away.

That was enough for me to believe. Fifty cents was enough for me to believe I could go across to the street to the corner by the pizza place everyone loved. Fifty cents was enough for me to go home and learn three more songs I knew people would recognize when they walked by. Fifty cents was enough for me to catch a glimpse of what I could become.

I would often be sitting on the corner in front of Pizza Sams in Midland, Michigan on a Friday or Saturday night. I learned how to navigate small crowds and interested listeners. Some nights I'd make a ton of money, some nights I wouldn't make much at all. I learned that street performers always put a few bucks in their own bucket, hat, or guitar case because no one wants to be the first to pull money out. Little trick I learned. You also didn't want to have too much money in your case because then people would think "oh, he's good, look at all that cash." You had to limit it to about fifteen visible dollars.

I went to different cities to sit on street corners and sing. Eventually getting to Times Square in New York, Boston, and Chicago. I loved being a street musician and I loved everything that came with it, all the interesting people, the flirtatious glances or interactions, buying a piece of pizza late at night with tip money. I was proud of my talent and proud to be stepping into the life I looked up to growing up.

Throughout college, as I studied music education to become a teacher, I would continue street performing but moved to more performances in coffee shops and small venues. When I neared graduation, I created my resume and proudly put "Street Performer 2005-present" in experience section.

"You are going to have to remove that," each professor and advisor would tell me.

"That's not professional experience and it's going to cost you opportunities."

Now listen, I take a lot of advice from great people – but I knew deep down that this was something I wanted schools to know about me. It said a lot about who I was. That I'm scrappy, that I can make really memorable and special moments without a ton of resources, that I think outside the box, that I am good with people.

Most of my professors and advisors were right, I had a lot of interviews that didn't pan out and all my friends were getting teaching jobs. I had interviewed lots of places and nothing was working out in my favor. I ended up at this tiny school in the center of Detroit for an interview. I don't know how else to say that the school was ghetto or hood besides saying it was a hood school. But in a beautiful way.

I sat in a room with three individuals who were not just educators, not just looking to fill a role in the school - you could tell that they were living for something bigger, part of something meaningful, and they were pillars in the community.

"Our students come with a lot Mr. Vercellino, many from single-parent homes, not a lot of fathers, lots of poverty; it's a tough place to work but a meaningful and wonderful community to be part of."

I handed them my resume.

"Oh you're a street musician? Can you tell us about that?"

This was the first school that asked about that section of my resume.

"It means I can make amazing things happen without much to work with, I know that much about myself."

"Well, that works out well because we have no budget for music, no fine arts department, no band room, no instruments, no flutes, or drums, or microphones…could you work with that?"

"Absolutely," I said, drawn to the challenge by my core.

I started that year with buckets, trash cans, pots and pans, and the world's shabbiest sound system. My classroom quickly became known for its creative output, our original songs, creative arrangements, and performances.

It was in this classroom, with dozens of talented and undervalued students, that I began to find the intersection of my deepest passion and the world's greatest needs. It was in this room that the bedrock of who I was as a teacher was formed. I rented a van and took 10 of my students street performing with me in a city an hour away. Someone donated a drum set to us and since no one could play the whole thing, we divided the individual drums up among the whole group. We used the $100 we made on the street to buy the biggest and most obnoxious ice cream cones at a local ice cream shop in Frankenmuth, MI.

It was at this school, my first-year teaching that I met and became friends with a little 5th grader named Tae Sosa who frequented my classroom with his little peanut-head and notebook. The same Tae Sosa whose artistry and lyrical sensations headline the nationally known performing group called, The Lion Heart Experience.

You never know where two quarters will take you and who you will meet along the way.

What is your two quarters moment?

CHAPTER 32

You Might Not Be Cut Out For This

"You might not be cut out for this type of work, Joe."

I sat across the principal of my school in a one-on-one meeting. I was in my 7th year teaching with a new school leader every year. I looked around this little office and recalled all the other years I sat across from a principal expressing their opinion on my skills as a teacher. They all quit.

"There's pilgrims and pioneers in education, Joe. Some are made to blaze a trail, they are adventurers, they are scrappy and tough – then there's others that come in behind them and settle where others have done the hard work."

She continued, "this is the wild-west, Joe. It's possible that this just might not be the place for you and that's ok."

Her name was Ms. Johnson.

I was made for this. It's just that this year kind of, sucked. I wish I had better words to describe it. Let me try.

My classroom was known for its musical output. Everything we did was original, and I was very proud of that. We wrote and recorded original songs that felt like radio hits to us. We collaborated with major producers and had all-star artists come and visit our classroom. If you were a student in my class, you knew this was not just a classroom, it was a platform that you could shoot off of into whatever type of future you want.

This specific year, in the middle of my 7th year teaching, it was rough. Behavior issues seemed never ending, parents were not only unsupportive, but felt hostile toward teachers. I had a group of 8th graders that somehow felt like had an agenda to "get me fired" for anything. Each day was a grind and struggle. It didn't help that the only time that an administrator would visit my classroom or reach out was for an observation or to check in on an issue. It was definitely not the year I felt like I was made to do what I do.

So here I was in my principal's office, going over our mid-year evaluation. She had given me the lowest and only low rating I had received as a teacher. "Ineffective, needs improvement." This would end up going on my public teaching record with the State of Michigan.

I wasn't sure what to say walking out of that meeting with her. I had to believe I was not ineffective; I was just struggling. My classroom was struggling. I was made to do this - so I continued. I continued offering the best I could as a teacher to my students and things did not turn around that year. I remember finishing the school year just grateful to have crawled across the finish line.

The next year started off really well, my students and I made and recorded a song for a local cola brand in Detroit called, Faygo. It received national attention and was featured on their website. I drove my minivan to their headquarters, and they loaded up my vehicle with enough pop for hundreds of students to enjoy: Rockin-Rye, Red-Pop, and Orange. We had another surprise that year - The principal who rated me ineffective, one day she didn't show up and we found out she just quit. Never to be seen again.

In other news, a year later I received The Teacher of The Year award for the City of Detroit. Not bad.

Here's why I wanted to share this story.

Only you know what you are made to do. Only you know what

you are here for. There's going to be people in your life, people of power and authority that are going to look at you in your face and tell you *I don't know if you're cut out for this.* There's going to be times in your life that you are going to be rated "ineffective, needs improvement." You are going to want to take that exit because you'll feel humiliated and alone.

> Only you know what you are made to do. Only you know what you are here for. There's going to be people in your life, people of power and authority that are going to look at you in your face and tell you I don't know if you're cut out for this.

Will you think of me sitting next to you in that moment? I'd love to rest my hand on your shoulder and give you a nod of reassurance that I am indeed here on the road with you, I know how it feels.

And friend, you hold on and continue to be the person you were made to be. The morning will follow the night. I'm so proud of you.

CHAPTER 33

Christmas Trees

When I was young there was a parking lot in my hometown that housed a large strip of businesses, a grocery store, a nail salon, a dollar store, party supplies, a karate studio, tax services, all the regular small-town businesses. In the wintertime there was a section of this parking lot where a small red shed would show up as it started to get cold. When mid-November arrived there would be Christmas trees that had been brought in for people to purchase. There were beautiful pines and blue ferns already cut and arranged in symmetrical rows for families to parous around and select the right tree for their home. Kids in hats and gloves would run up and down the aisles of trees. At nighttime, strung lights up above would illuminate the selection of Christmas trees. You would see dads throwing the trees onto their car roofs and tying them down with twine.

Our Christmas tree would almost droop with the weight of all the Christmas ornaments from my six siblings and I. Bulbs and strings of lights, school pictures surrounded by glued macaroni noodles on cut-out paper plates. A tiny pickle ornament that we all loved. It was all there. It all hung on the tree.

Christmas would come, snow would cover the ground. I would wake up at 6:00 AM at the latest to look at the presents and soak in the morning - finding it so hard to believe that my parents were still sleeping!

One of my favorite gifts growing up was a treasure chest, just like the ones in pirate movies I had seen. I would fill it up with all my most valuable items and lock it – I kept the chest for most of my life. My second favorite gift was a piano keyboard I had asked my parents for just a few days before Christmas. I don't know where they found it, but they did, and I loved mixing sounds and creating music on that keyboard.

On Christmas each year, we would take turns traveling to my cousin's house, which was about two hours away. After our morning opening presents, we would bundle up, load into our family van, and head out of town.

Right before getting onto the highway, we would pass the parking lot by the grocery store, next to the nail salon, dollar store, party supplies, karate studio and tax services. In the parking lot was a red shed and on Christmas day, I would press my head against the glass of the van, rubbing away the frost that accumulated meeting the heat of the van and the frigid temperatures outside together on the window. I would look out to see the 10-15 trees that were still sitting out there in the parking lot. There were no more symmetrical rows. The leftover trees, some notably skinnier or misshapen, bent at the top, they all stood in their own space in the parking lot. There were no people. The buzz of the holiday had migrated to individual homes.

I would look out to see the 10-15 trees that were still sitting out there in the parking lot. There were no more symmetrical rows. The leftover trees, some notably skinnier or misshapen, bent at the top, they all stood in their own space in the parking lot.

This small passing moment each year revealed an interesting part of my personality. From people to objects, from animals to trees – I have a soft spot and sensitivity for the last, the lost, the least, and the looked over. Trees do not have feelings, that I know of, but I felt bad that these pines had been cut down, propped up to be taken home by a family and ascend to (as far as I would think) it's most glorified state of being the centerpiece of a holiday, draped in tinsel, lights, bearing the weight of an entire family's generation of ornaments. But not these trees. They were removed from the ground for no reason at all it seems. Never to be decorated or illuminated, never to have presents fill the space beneath their branches. These trees would just be removed and disposed of.

Friend, I wonder if any of you reading this find yourself touched by moments that do not matter much to others? I am curious what beautiful part of your personality it reveals about the way you move and take in the world around you.

I have an eye for any that are the last, the lost, the least, or the looked over. I do not like to see people alone or passed over. I do not like to see the anxious look of isolation or fear in others' eyes. I feel deeply when I hear that someone cannot find a place where they belong.

How about you?

A few weeks ago, I got off stage after speaking at a school about identity and self-worth. I met a young man in tears as he walked up to me with his arms open.

"I needed this so bad..." he said through coughing and muffled tears that were now soaking into my shoulder.

He didn't have any friends behind him. I couldn't help but notice after this hug that there was no one to walk with this guy back to class with an arm over the shoulder. It was just him and I.

"I can't tell you how much this meant to me, I'm so happy, I needed this so much, I'm so happy..."

"I know," I said softly to him in this embrace. "We all need this don't we?"

Today, in this small moment in the high school lobby – the last got to the front of the line. The lost was embraced. The least recognized their value and the looked over was seen for a moment. One of those bent and misshapen trees was picked to go home and be what it was meant to be. There's still a lot of them out there.

CHAPTER 34

Don't Send Another Text, Joe

"How is the day feeling today, Joe? What's been on your mind that you'd like to talk about?" My therapist Jackson asked me from across the small room.

"Texting," I said.

"I love it," he said gesturing me to expand my thought.

Let me explain it to you like I explained it to Jackson. At the time of this therapy session, I was leading a non-profit in the city of Detroit. We had a fantastic group of students that we had been with for years and years, we got to see them grow and be part of crucial developments in their lives. Helping students earn their driver's license, open bank accounts, learn to get and keep a job; really exciting things if none of those really exist in your family for you to observe growing up. We also had a solid group of leaders within the organization, people who love the students and put effort into their success as well.

Celebrating others is really important to me. Every couple of days I'd send a text like this to our group chat; "Hey! I just wanted to shout out Rodrigo (leader) for helping out Dante (student) the other day. Dante had a flat tire, and it was so kind of Rodrigo to go help him out. Dante told me he was so glad he wasn't alone having his first flat tire."

"Perfect," Jackson said nodding his head tracking with my story. "That sounds great."

"Right, except no one responds to the text, Jackson! No one types anything back, no acknowledgment whatsoever, like everyone is way too busy to take two seconds to respond."

"Don't send another text, Joe. Not until you can really be the person sending that text. Don't send another celebratory text when your underlying goal is to just teach everyone a lesson."

Jackson looks at me visibly upset by this.

There are 15 other leaders in this group chat, no one has time to respond back and say something small like "Wow, great job!" or "Proud of you Rodrigo" or "I love that, that's what we are all about." Just nothing. Not even a like on the text.

"I know the leaders see this text, Jackson!" I say to my therapist with passion and annoyance. "How hard is it to just acknowledge someone? Everyone is constantly on their phone, yet not one person can at least say "cool." Just, nothing.

Jackson asked me, "Does anyone else ever put a celebration in the texting thread?"

"Yes!" I said.

"Just the other day Noelle (a leader) sent some pictures from a hangout with some of the students and said it went really well and it was great relational time."

"So, what did you do?" Jackson asked me politely from his chair.

"I responded back right away, I typed something like 'that's awesome, thanks so much for sharing! I love this. Keep it up."

"Tell me why you chose to do that," Jackson responded.

"Well, it's obviously awesome that they had such a great time with the students, but I really want the people in the text to see how easy it is to just freaking acknowledge someone, it takes three seconds, literally."

"Was your goal to celebrate this person or to teach everyone a lesson?" Jackson said. "If you can answer me honestly, what was the real motive for your text, why did you send it? Why did you send it, really?"

"Truthfully," I said. "I sent it because I want to show them how easy it is to just freaking acknowledge someone's text."

"Don't send another text, Joe. Not until you can really be the person sending that text. Don't send another celebratory text when your underlying goal is to just teach everyone a lesson."

"Then I won't reply to anything!" I said equally sarcastically and truthfully.

This was a good growth moment for me. It both gave me permission and challenged me to not play the part without being the person. It was eating me up inside. Twisting my stomach and my mind with anger.

Before I send a text now, especially to celebrate someone or acknowledge someone I stop and pause to ask myself if I am 100% committed to sincerely celebrating this person or acknowledging them – because if I am I will not be concerned with anyone else's reply or lack of reply.

Any time you are playing the part without being the person, my friend, it's going to take you to a horrible place. Maybe not now, but soon.

CHAPTER 35

Lion Heart Vocabulary: Face Mask Moment

I was watching a football game on TV. Honestly, similar to our production engineer Jeremiah - I think I enjoy the atmosphere around football the most. The noise of the game, lounging on the couch, funny commercials, good food. On this day I was catching the end of the Army vs. Navy[11] game. Of course, they are rivals and there's a lot of pressure on both teams to win this game. I'm not particularly invested in the outcome but I'm here for the atmosphere around the sport. If there's queso and chips, I'll watch any game you want.

Both teams were in double overtime for the first time in their history playing each other. As time was winding down, the Navy was only inches away from the endzone. One of their star running backs, Anthony Hall, plunged through a wall of Army football players to cross the threshold to the endzone. In these final seconds, as he stretched for the goal line, the ball was knocked out of his hands - resulting in a fumble recovered by the Army, driven down the field. With only moments to go, Hall watched from the sideline as the Navy defense tried to prevent the drive from the Army down to the endzone. The Army drove the ball down the field and got within distance to kick a game-winning field goal.

I found the camerawork the most intriguing. As the players lined up for this field goal, the cameras would cut back to Hall on the sideline, standing in nervous anticipation, knowing if he would not have fumbled the other team would not have the ball ready to kick this point to win the game. You could see on Hall's face *please miss, please miss, please miss.*

It was too late. There was too much momentum. Too much strength and not enough time. The kicker for the Army, Quinn Maretzki, sent the ball soaring straight through both goal posts to win the game in the last milliseconds of play.

The camera cut back to Hall. ESPN's coverage of the moment reads like this; "Hall collapsed to the ground with his face in his hands."

I stood up from the couch hoping the camera would stay on Hall. Everything I see is through the lens of identity and self-worth, I had to see how those around him would react to the moment Hall was in. You could see that the entire weight of the loss was on his shoulders, and he was bent under the weight of feeling he had lost the game for the team.

I am not a good football player; I know all the basics though. I am intrigued by one dynamic of the game I always like to watch - it's when a coach grabs a player by the facemask with one hand, forces their gaze straight ahead, and imparts words the player has no choice but to take in and conform to.

"Grab his face mask!" I found myself yelling at the game on the Television. "Someone grab this man's face mask and tell him life is bigger than this game, life is bigger than this moment!"

I should have been a football coach. I'm not sure I would coach the winningest team, but I would absolutely coach the most emotionally aware team.

I talk to coaches all around the country and ask them if they ever do a team meeting where they ask their players how they internalize a loss? The answer is usually something like *"never thought of that before."*

Both wins and losses are formative experiences. They are moments pregnant with potential that deserve more than "We'll get them next time" or "You played good tonight fellas."

Back to Hall, the running back for the Navy.

I desperately wanted to reach through the screen and reach this man. Like Hall, there are many of us walking through life bent over and collapsed emotionally from pressure, from shame, from failure, from disappointment and we need a facemask moment.

We need someone to force our gaze upward, we need someone to grab us by the shoulders and say "Snap out of it! I'm here with you, life is bigger than this moment." We need someone to push us a little further. We need someone to grab us by the facemask and say, "Get up, you are not a failure."

The team and I in The Lion Heart Experience offer these moments to each other. I have been grateful for the times that Tae or Jeremiah have pulled me out of despair or anxiousness. We were at a school one time where a particular staff member had an unfortunate and misunderstood interaction with me. I could see her walking around the room to other staff complaining about our group (mostly me), pointing over our way. We had a show in 10 minutes, and I was flushed with emotion, I want people to like me, I want people to like us, we are good people doing good work. Tae looked at me and put his hands on my shoulders, "V, screw them, let's do what we do best, you are going to kill it out there."

I'm not here to endorse that wording in-particular but I needed a face mask moment. We had another time in Texas where we found ourselves at odds with an auditorium manager. I could not focus; I was overwhelmed with frustration and anger. I sat in the green room wondering how I was going to transition to an uplifting presence in the room. Jeremiah came back to the green room and in front of the team, put his hands on my shoulders and said something along the lines of "Hey, we have a show, we will get past this, let's get out there and give a great performance, life is bigger than this moment, get up."

My friend, may you experience a beautiful handful of facemask moments from people around you that care about you not giving into the low-functioning emotions. May you understand when it's your turn to force that gazes upwards as well.

CHAPTER 36

Tori

A few months ago, we went to a high school in southwest Michigan. We started with a middle school show that went really well! In the front row there were three high school students that sat and watched, they were part of a cohort for high school students who wanted to be future teachers. They had spent part of the year gaining experience working with the middle school students in the room.

One of these high school students was Tori.

After our first show she lingered in the lobby, sitting alone on a bench on her phone. She was small with short blonde hair, ripped jeans, and a dark top. We asked her if she'd like to come eat lunch with us as we sat in the atrium of the school with our sandwiches. She walked over and we spent the next half hour learning about her life. She was vibrant and proud. So ahead in all of her classes that her teachers didn't mind if she wasn't even in attendance. She was a top performer in her choir class. She knew everyone's name. Her life felt like it was straight out of an overcoming story in a movie. One parent in jail, one parent dead from suicide, living with her grandparents. The primary caretaker of her 1st grade brother - anticipating the release of her uncle from a mental care facility as he suffered from dementia. With all this she was poised to graduate and go to college to become a teacher.

Over our two days at this school, Tori was with us everywhere. She ate with us, walked with us, performed with us on stage. She brought me a handwritten note on the last day with a school hat to fit in with the purple and white school spirit.

I told her when she graduates to call us and come work with us in The Lion Heart Experience. Her warmth, kindness, and her story would be a wonderful platform to reach lots of kids like her who had to navigate through hardship too early in life.

She was resilient and bright and beautiful.

One of the tough things about our job is going to a school, making beautiful connections with students, and returning to the school a year later not to see some of their faces. The number of students that fall victim to rates of suicide each year is staggering, it's impact immense and emotional.

One of the tough things about our job is going to a school, making beautiful connections with students, and returning to the school a year later not to see some of their faces. The number of students that fall victim to rates of suicide each year is staggering, it's impact immense and emotional.

Tori was one of these students. Just two months after meeting her and sharing a very special two days, I found out she had taken her life one night. It was the type of news that left me breathless for a few minutes, a flurry of anger, confusion, and deep sadness. Her profile on Instagram still vibrant and encouraging like she was still here. *What in the world, Tori? What the heck, I had no idea the pressures of life were too much...*

Tae has a song called pain and purpose. Truly, in the evening I heard that news I was at the corner of pain and purpose. It's for people like Tori that we exist.

Life matters, my friends.

I got lots of messages from students on social media letting me know Tori had left us. They all worded the news their own way, but one common phrase surfaced in each message. *"I don't know why, but she loved you guys and what you stand for."*

I know why. Life has value. Beautiful value.

From the teen trying to fit in, balancing the hardships of life and loss like Tori, or the dad lost in his career holding both the celebration of achievement in one hand and the crushing weight of depression in the other, like me - life has value.

Whether it is life that has had the chance to mature, develop, formed through the hands of experience, emotion, love, and loss or the life developing inside of a mother's body at six weeks with measurable brain waves and a beating heart. The life matters.

This is what Tori felt. Seen. Heard. Celebrated. A feeling many of us will chase our whole life.

Largely, schools do not really know how to handle student suicide. I don't blame them. They want to create a space for students to process the death and hurt and confusion but don't want to force anything in fear of triggering other students. They have the judgmental eyes and opinions of parents afraid that any move will be too much or not enough in the face of the tragedy.

Tori. If I would have known - how I wish I would have checked in again. And one more time to see how you are doing carrying the weight of your life. But now, we live on at the corner of pain and purpose, looking for more who are like you. In hopes that one day they may taste a real sense of belonging and hope. This one's for you.

Crying

I am not much of a crier.

I always feel weird about that statement. When I say it. When I hear other people say it. My kids are criers, I don't know if they would "identify" as criers - but they cry a lot. When they are physically hurt, when they are emotionally hurt, if their little sister takes their toy, if mommy and daddy (me) are the most unfair and mean parents 'in the whole wide world.' They cry. Jeremiah, our audio engineer, he talks about having a good cry and part of me wishes I could cry more and felt the need to cry more. Julie and Olivia, both Lion Heart crew members - they both talk about crying all the time.

I do get choked up when I see videos like extreme makeover home edition when a family gets a new home, I tear up when I see moms and dads reunited with their kids, the military videos - it's never a full-on cry though.

The best tears, the warm, unbridled tears, the overwhelming sense of beauty and belonging overflowing in my body. I've only experienced it once and it was the most euphoric 10 minutes of my life.

Let me say this, as you are getting to know me. I love being married. I love my wife, Heather. I love the finality of marriage, that *this. is. it.* There's no more guess work or wondering if this is the right person for me or if this conflict is going to break us up. We are forsaking anything that could have been with anyone else for this person. All in.

Heather is my number one supporter, friend, and encouragement in all areas of my life. I am fiercely involved in supporting, loving, and helping her develop as well. She is a luxury designer here in Detroit and our kids know, mom makes houses beautiful. I love that our kids get to see mom so alive in her passion, so artistic, so invigorated – and I love that they know that mom and dad are best friends.

In our marriage, we do not even utter the word divorce. There's no having one of us sleep on the couch because of anger. There's no name calling or storming out and driving away in a vehicle if someone is mad. We protect our relationship because it means so much to both of us. Now, do not get me wrong here. Marriage is the hardest thing I've ever done – it is hard work – it is also the most worthwhile thing I've ever invested in. It's hard to describe. It would be like trying to tell you what tasting honey is like or smelling a rose, you must experience it to identify with it. If you and your friend join us over here, my wife and I will be cheering you on.

It was not always like that though.

Let me give you a little back story on Heather and I. Girls will love this little chapter, by the way.

I met Heather when I was a senior in college, I was on my way out. In fact, I was on an extra-senior year because I had failed some important classes and needed to retake them. I had not dated anyone in a couple years and the last break-up I went through I told myself "I don't want to experience this again." It hurt so bad; it was such a mess. It's just the worst, you know what I mean?

After that relationship I tried to be very intentional about my interactions with girls and figure out if something was the real deal or a passing crush. I developed some self-control within that couple year span when it came to my connections with the opposite sex.

One day, my friend told me about this freshman girl. Now, I will say this. I wasn't seeing anyone, but I did know that I was a catch. I just didn't want to mess around, especially with a freshman in college.

My dear reader, I don't think you should be bashful about this either. If you're a catch, you're good looking and responsible, you've got dreams and talent and value. Own that.

Anyway, I heard about this freshman girl. I lived in a house with eight other guys, and we would invite people over for dinner regularly. On this particular evening my roommates made ravioli and this girl was going to come over with one of our mutual friends for dinner. I did not think much of this dinner until Heather walked through the door. Her soft brown eyes were mesmerizing to me behind her blonde side bangs. I did not want to talk to anyone else at dinner, she immediately intrigued and captivated me. I also thought she was kind of hot because she was on probation, she was a bad girl, and I was a pastor's kid.

She was a cheerleader at the university we went to. I didn't like football, but I'd be with all those guys with their chests painted at games in early December. I was there to pretend to like football and to not pretend to be fully into one specific cheerleader.

Over the course of a couple years, we developed a relationship that felt like home. I told her I loved her, and she loved me. I left college and started teaching in Detroit at the school that I would meet Tae Sosa at.

We dated long distance for three years. I would drive up on weekends to go see her. As she neared the end of college experience there was a natural pivot into a season of Heather wondering where is this going? A lot of our friends were getting married. She was going to graduate soon. I remember one wedding where Heather and I both stood in the wedding party looking across at each other. The overwhelming thought of marriage kind of terrified me, I didn't think about it much because I was teaching in Detroit, and she was finishing school three hours away.

One day Heather sat me down, "Joe." Heather said looking at me intently. With an equal amount of love and weariness – "where is our relationship going? We've been dating over three years…" I wish I answered her back with swift conviction, but to be honest, I didn't have much direction. It was not good.

"I'm going to be a bride, Joe." She paused. "I'm not going to be a long-term girlfriend; I'm going to be a bride and if it's with you – that's amazing. If our relationship is not headed that way, I deserve to know that as well, I'm not going to waste my time."

She continued, "You need to take some time to figure this out, don't tell me you love me anymore until you can tell me where our relationship is headed."

She was right. I was terrified but my respect for Heather Huntley went way up. This is a girl who knows what she wants and what she deserves. I did need to figure out what was going on, she deserved direction and intention. That sent me into the most intense personal time of reflection of my life. I remember sitting with my uncle Andrew, who is a wonderful mentor to me.

"Can you just tell me if she's the one or not?" I remember asking him. "Like, what do you think?"

"All I can tell you, Joe, is not to make any decisions out of fear. Don't stay with her because you are afraid to break-up, and don't break-up because you are afraid of the commitment. Just don't make a decision out of fear," and he took a bite of his jelly toast. He had it all figured out anyway, he had been married to my aunt (who is wonderful) for 20 years and had four kids. How did he figure out my aunt was the one? Isn't everyone supposed to have a "this is the one" moment?

After a couple weeks, I emerged with a single thought – like a voice speaking to me.

*Joe, you are very focused on wondering if she's the one. The real question is, are you willing and are you ready to **be** the one.*

I took a few of my students with me to pick out a ring for Heather and surprised her on a rooftop with her roommates in Chicago. I decided to say yes. Yes to Heather, yes to commitment, Yes to faithfulness…Luckily she said yes too ;)

Nine months later we got married and I experienced warm, beautiful tears for the first time. When Heather walked down the aisle, she took my breath away. Her faithfulness and belief in me, her strength and wisdom and her physical beauty. I thought that there was no moment where I could love her more.

A couple years into our marriage, Heather and I were expecting our first child. We did not know if we were having a girl or a boy, it was going to be a surprise for both of us. When my son was born, they placed him on Heather's chest. Sitting next to her, I was overwhelmed in the most beautiful way. Tears streamed down my face and love filled my heart for this tiny little combination of my wife and I, our son Elias. Motherhood bloomed right in front of me and my friend, my wife, became a beautiful mother. I walked out to the waiting room and could not even speak as my own mom and dad embraced me.

When my son was born, they placed him on Heather's chest. Sitting next to her, I was overwhelmed in the most beautiful way. Tears streamed down my face and love filled my heart for this tiny little combination of my wife and I, our son Elias.

"I have a son" I managed to trickle across my lips in a flood of beautiful, overwhelming, warm tears.

I have learned in my relationship with Heather that our marriage is a mysterious and beautiful process of becoming and being *the one*. Each experience we go through shapes us toward each other. Things are good over here, my friends. Marriage is the best and it gets sweeter and deeper with time as we continually discover each other in each season. I wish I cried more often - This girl has brought the most beautiful tears down across my cheeks. Thank you, Heather, I love being here with you.

CHAPTER 38

Tap In

Tae had these really dope shirts to sell for one of his singles, "Mind over Matter." We hired one of the best graffiti artists in Detroit to sketch up this mean, ripped gorilla (Tae's emoji of choice), with a sideways hat. The shirts were cool. Exclusive. Flashy. Unique. We worked out a deal in hopes that the shirt sales would create a nice stream of profit for Tae.

It wasn't long before we had some good marketing going, graphics, photos to start moving the shirts. Tae posted on his Instagram the epic Mind over Matter T-shirt and the reposts started flooding in. I'd click on his story and see friends and family who had reposted the shirt.

"Tap in with Tae Sosa"

"Check out Brodies merch"

"Go support my man and get you a shirt"

"Get right with the new merch!"

"Yo! Check out what nephew is doing"

(fire emoji fire emoji fire emoji)

(Comment, comment, comment, share, share, share)

In my head, I was thinking Tae was taking all types of orders from friends and family. The buzz was electric. So many shares and comments and likes and reposts.

"Sold any shirts Tae?" I asked him one day.

"Not really," he responded. "Just one to my aunt, I was so surprised when she bought one"

We both sat and nodded at each other slowly.

"That's how it goes," I said as we grinned sharing an honest and truthful moment with each other.

What does real love and belief and support look like? For a lot of us young people I'm afraid that most of us have fallen for a cheap knock-off version.

What does real love and belief and support look like? For a lot of us young people I'm afraid that most of us have fallen for a cheap knock-off version. It looks like love, support and belief, it sounds like love and support, for a second it feels like belief until it disappears off our timeline.

Tae felt this when he put his shirts up for sale and everyone reposted and told *everyone else* to "tap-in" with Tae Sosa and grab a shirt while Tae sat and couldn't help but notice that he still had a full box of shirts and no money in his hands.

For me, as a related personal experience - my mind always goes to Giving Tuesday; the Tuesday after Black Friday where everyone is urged to give to a non-profit as a way of countering all the personal shopping done on black Friday.

For eight years I ran a non-profit in the city of Detroit. We did really great work in the lives of students, helping to shift generational momentum and providing incredible growth opportunities. Like all non-profits, we were always in need of money to continue the programming, the work, and keep the lights and heat on for our facility. It was stressful to say the least.

On Giving Tuesday, I would get on Facebook and notice the good amount of people who had posted about us as a non-profit worthy of support on Giving Tuesday. I'd see things like *"please consider giving to Shiloh Detroit this Tuesday."* I'd see our leaders posting pictures of themselves with students from the non-profit with a heartwarming story and a request to give at the end.

At the end of the day, I couldn't help but notice the bank account had not changed at all – Everyone had endorsed the heck out of the non-profit but none of them actually gave anything.

I'm sitting next to Tae with his box of shirts.

I'm sure you have your own experience related to this.

Real support is not shares, likes, comments, or posts. Real support is not hype.

Real support is tangible.
Real support buys a T-shirt THEN tells others to do the same.
Real support gives to the non-profit THEN asks if others would join.

Real support does not play the part without being the person. That phrase has been a bit of a theme weaving through this book.

If you want to know who really believes in you… better yet, if you want to show someone you really believe in them, give them the best of your time, your talent, and your resources. Offer the best of your time, not left-over time to assist them, encourage them, and help them build. Give the best of your talents and your gifts to help them out. Lastly, put your money where your mouth is and invest your finances into the person, with or without telling the world that you did it.

Get in front of their face, put your hand on their shoulder, and tell them you are proud of them and why you are proud of them.

This is what real belief and support looks like. When it is applied it changes the world. Most of us get too caught up in looking like we support something – I know we can do better.

Someone buy a T-shirt and tell Tae I sent you.

CHAPTER 39

The Elliptical

About a year and a half ago I started going to the gym. Planet Fitness to be precise! It's big and purple and yellow everywhere. NO JUDGMENT ZONE wallpaper plastered on the wall. There's an alarm that goes off if you are showing off, dropping weights, or grunting while you lift. Inside the entrance there's huge 4-foot letters that say YOU BELONG!

Yes, complete with the exclamation point for emphasis. Just in case you weren't told you belong, you **do**. I see "You belong" signs in the three places people feel the most left out (schools, churches, and gyms). That's not a knock on any of them, it just seems like overcompensating a bit when YOU BELONG is right in your face. Belonging is a feeling; you can't communicate it in size 788 font or bold letters, and you don't feel more belonging if there's an exclamation point at the end of the word. You can't communicate belonging on a poster, in bright neon-lettering, by whispering or yelling it in someone's face. It's something you feel, or you don't.

> Belonging is a feeling; you can't communicate it in size 788 font or bold letters, and you don't feel more belonging if there's an exclamation point at the end of the word.

I digress.

Back to the gym. This is about my vantage point in this spectacular grape and honey, judgement-free place of belonging – the elliptical machine. Home base for me. If you don't know what an elliptical machine is, it is the least work out, workout machine created. You stand and place your hands on long ski-like poles, you glide as your legs swing back and forth. At times you wonder if the machine is moving your legs on its own. After 30 minutes I get off the machine, not sweating, no elevated heart rate and convince myself that I had worked out.

As I stand, gliding on the elliptical, I scan the gym. I move my eyes from the Food Network television to people watching (careful not to judge so I do not offend the wallpaper). There are all types of people here. There's the rather large uncle-looking person who, I think, is here with his nephew today trying to get him in shape. Uncle looks a little bit like a jelly-filled donut today. There is the guy who wears the blue-tooth headphones that illuminate to the music as he dances from machine to machine. Everyone has headphones in. My friend Gene walks by – a man with dark skin, red and green hair split down the middle, and bright hazel-colored contacts that make him look out of a suspense thriller movie. I nod my head, smile, and wave at Gene. There's the guy who is shadow boxing while he walks backward on the treadmill. All types of people are here, and I am gliding, "ellipticaling" as I figure out what workout to do next.

As I scan the room, knowing I do not know much about weights or form – I watch other people. I watch guys who are buff and make mental notes in my head to *do what they are doing next but don't make it obvious.* After my elliptical workout and after they have moved on, I go over there and copy them. It must be working for them, I think to myself.

My current workout routine is a collage of things I've picked up from watching people who are more in shape, toned, and fit than I am. I watch them (from afar in a non-judgmental, full of belonging way). When they walk away, I swim through the purple and yellow machines, and I copy what I saw.

As I was lifting, I was thinking about an interaction I had with a friend where they told me about some money advice they had gotten from their uncle.

"My uncle said that as long as someone owes you, you'll be rich."

"Is your uncle rich?" I asked.

"No, he's broke," my friend said.

Why take any money advice from your uncle if he's broke, I thought.

I look down at my phone and scroll through Instagram for a moment while I rest between lifting sets. A parenting advice post, I scroll through the horizontal posts and can't help but think (as a parent of three kids) that there's no way this was written by an actual parent; this sounds like someone who does not have kids. Frustrated, I put the phone down and begin my next set.

While I'm doing my next set of chest presses I think back on a conversation I had with another young person that I mentor, Dion, who got some recent relationship advice from his parent.

Trying my best in my thoughts to abide by the no-judgment zone wallpaper, I can feel my annoyed conscious reflecting back on this moment and thinking in my head, *Your parent has yet to be in a relationship that does not turn into an absolute train wreck, why are you taking advice from your parent?*

This is not uncommon. Let me help simplify this and give you some action steps.

Do not take advice about cars from someone who doesn't have a car. Ruined all their cars. Or who's car is in terrible shape.

Do not take dating advice from someone who goes from toxic relationship to toxic relationship.

Do not take money advice from broke people.

Do not take life-balance advice from someone who is constantly stressed and over-extended.

Our daily lives are inundated with all types of advice, thousands of messages a day from Instagram, TikTok, people in our lives, commercials, ads – all of them telling you how to make money, how to improve your love life, and how to find inner-peace.

Friend, would you like to join me on the elliptical?
From where you are right now, can you locate someone around you that is living the way you would like to live? They are financially successful, and you'd like to be where they are. Do you know someone who has a great relationship with their spouse or kids, and you'd like to have the type of connection they have with your girlfriend or boyfriend, husband, or wife? Have you interacted with someone who just seems to exude peace, calmness, and control?

Watch them. When you're done on the elliptical, go get some reps in the same way they do.

If you want to be braver than I am, go talk to them and ask them *"Can I learn from you, I'd like to grow in the areas you seem to be successful at?"*

See you in the gym.

CHAPTER 40

I Should Have Punched You, Dan

My eyes filled up with tears instead. Hot tears, the ones ready to burst and roll down your cheeks. The tears that beg other teens to point and laugh because I was caught between embarrassment and physical pain. In the moment it felt like shoving you down to the ground wasn't even an option. I guess that is why we grow, if you tried that again - you would get all the smoke. I'm not the same person you tripped in 9th grade. I couldn't even comprehend how mean you were.

I made a conversation deck, it's a little tan box with 109 interesting questions to ask the people around you. Some of them are questions that have created the most interesting conversations in The Lion Heart crew at our dinners, some are questions I love to ask other people or questions that I also love to answer. For about six months I kept an open note in my phone, and I would record interesting questions I heard, saw, or thought of until I turned them into a deck of cards and put them in a box. These cards are available on our website and on our app if you want to check them out.

One of these questions is this:
"Has there ever been a time where you should have punched someone and you didn't?"

I've never been in a physical fight, nothing serious outside of shoving when I was a kid – but no fists, no blood. Maybe I'm lucky? Maybe not. I lean toward the maybe not more because there's a part of myself that I do not know and I don't like that. A part of myself that hasn't been expressed and I don't know who I will be when (or if) I'm in a place or situation where getting physical is the only real option.

Part of the reason I do not know this part of myself is because fighting was always taught to me as a last resort and that it's always better to walk away than to engage. It makes me a very interested question asker when I talk to Tae Sosa or Jeremiah (Lion Heart Production) about their experiences and upbringing since they both have had to pull out their hands once or twice.

This question though, "has there ever been a time where you should have punched someone and you didn't?" has a definite answer for me though. I know the exact memory and the answer is, "Yes. I should have punched you, Dan."

In 9th grade I was on the basketball team, I was giving it another shot after my 8th grade season in hopes that something about high school would offer me a competitive boost. Maybe I'd be more aggressive in 9th grade than I was in 8th. There were definitely higher stakes in high school basketball. In the very least, it wouldn't be at all bad if a cute girl came to watch one of your games. I had a goal!

I was not much different in 9th grade than I was in 8th. A little taller, a weird poofy haircut where I had put a natural bleach called sun-in on the top of my head to make it lighter. My teammates were not very kind and made it clear to me that things hadn't changed since 8th grade. There was one guy on my team named Dan, who seemed to really enjoy finding ways to poke fun at me. Little snickers, side comments, or complaints about me messing up a play would usually result in me just pretending I didn't hear even though deep down it stung a little bit.

One day during practice we were scrimmaging each other before a game the next day. I was running down the court to get back on defense and Dan was on offense, he was also booking it down to the other end. As I took off down the court Dan ran behind me and kicked my back foot to the side really hard, forcing me to trip and fall forward and I face planted onto the floor hard. The game stopped for a second while Dan snickered, "he can't even run right" and my teammates laughed.

I felt so embarrassed. I couldn't even comprehend the intentionality behind why he did that. I was stunned as I got up, my wrists buzzing with pain while I lifted myself off the floor. I was his teammate – I wanted him to be a great player, I just wanted to practice and that's it – I was fine with the physical aggression that happened in regular play, but I couldn't even wrap my head around intentionally tripping your teammate while they are running.

My eyes filled up with tears instead. Hot tears, the ones ready to burst and roll down your cheeks. The tears that beg other teens to point and laugh because you are caught between embarrassment and physical pain.

The coach gave his best "alright, alright, let's play fair" and restarted the scrimmage.

In the moment it felt like shoving Dan down to the ground wasn't even an option. Only to take it. Where was my gut reflex to stand up for myself? For honor. Why didn't I get up and say, "I'm not the one" and tackle him to the ground?

I guess that is why we grow.

I've learned from Tae Sosa that sometimes you have to be physical as a strong message to the people around you that there are things that don't fly, lines you don't cross, things you are not allowed to say, ways you cannot touch. Malcolm Gladwell talks about this cultural dynamic in his book "outliers" as a culture of honor.

There was nothing wrong in my upbringing, with having so much emphasis on being nice, gentle, understanding, forgiving, and patient – but with that said, I parent my son differently. He's nice and gentle and understanding and forgiving and patient – but he's also familiar with the phrases I've picked up from my time in the city.

"You don't want these hands, you don't want the smoke." I tell Eli, that no one pushes you around. If they do, you shove them down as hard as you can. If someone touches your sister, they need to get a "buzz down" (thanks Jaylin), there's no "hey don't touch my sister," you need to pull out the hands, son.

When I look into my son's eyes, I see myself. A kind person who needed permission to be physical. I think that I would have learned to love myself more by recognizing that I'm strong, protective, and can be dangerous as well, but I never got there.

Now, I live in expectation. I do not go looking for a fight anywhere, but I am sensitive to never return the version of myself that can be tripped and embarrassed... and quiet... trying to tap into the idea that my kindness is my strength.

> When I look into my son's eyes, I see myself. A kind person who needed permission to be physical. I think that I would have learned to love myself more by recognizing that I'm strong, protective, and can be dangerous as well, but I never got there.

I should have punched you in the face, Dan.

For me.

I wish I gave you all the smoke. I think we would have both been better off in the end.

CHAPTER 41

Everyone Will Know My Name

One day, my freshman year of high school I was at the mall with my dad picking up some gifts for Christmas. We took a small break to eat lunch in the food court. I always loved the breadsticks at Sbarro Pizza, a New-York style chain that had the best buttery parmesan garlic breadsticks. We sat together at a table, I took a bite of my breadstick and watched all types of people walk by in and out of the mall.

"I want to come back here someday and have everyone know my name, Dad. One day I'll be famous."

My dad, known for his honesty and integrity responded back with love, "Well, that sounds like a selfish and self-centered ambition," through his slice of peperoni and he continued to eat.

I felt bad, I guess it was selfish. I tried to get rid of that feeling. I still didn't really know what to do with it though. I just felt like I needed to say it.

Years later, something about this moment would resurface in a wildly different context and change the way I would see everything about this experience and buttery breadsticks.

Ten years after that experience with my cheesy breadstick and selfish dream I found myself in my first teaching job at my first school in inner-city Detroit. I was the only white guy in the room. Beautiful black and brown faces would fill my music class each day – I began to learn about and be accepted by a new culture that intrigued me and brought out new parts of my personality I didn't know were there.

In this classroom I had a student, a 14-year-old who seemed to make it his mission each day to refuse to follow any of my instructions to the class. It felt like immediate friction and resistance to even the smallest direction. There was no work getting done, this young person would even refuse to move from his seat. He had it in his mind that I needed to learn that he would not be controlled or directed.

I remember sitting across from this young man in a one-on-one conversation. I was perplexed. I did not have anything against him. I had observed from him that actually he was very fun and easy going with his friends, but he was bent on defying me.

"I'm not against you," I said to him gently. "I am just a first-year teacher trying my best to run this classroom smoothly in a way that we all learn and have a good time doing that. It seems any direction I give you refuse or do the opposite."

He looked away from me in protest. I was stuck.

And for some reason, my parmesan garlic cheesy breadstick from Sbarro came back to me.

In about five seconds my brain rewired itself, memories and feelings that floated freely inside of me locked into place, and I came to a realization that expressed itself in these words to my protesting student.

"I like your defiance," I said to him. He furrowed his eyebrows, surprised or disgusted, glanced at me then back to the wall.

"I like the way you dig in your heels and refuse to back down. I love that about your personality."

He did the same thing he did before, but this time dropped his shoulders a touch, still keeping his arms protectively crossed and looked in a different direction.

"I just think you might be misapplying this gift you have, buddy. You have the gift of not backing down, you are strong and stubborn and that is actually, amazing. There are people in this world that need someone like you to stand up for them, to say no more to oppressors, to refuse to buckle under pressure, to be immovable. There are people out there that need you. That is who you are and that is beautiful and strong."

I continued, "here's the thing man, I'm not an enemy, I'm for you – and I don't want you to stop being what you are – arms crossed, defiant, strong and immovable – I just want you to find the right context to exercise it in. I bet you would be an amazing lawyer someday, you never give up in an argument with me, you are so fierce and sharp and quick. You would be amazing at that…"

It took some time, but I ended up having a healthy and meaningful connection with this student and I also improved the relationship I had with a 15-year-old version of me that only exists in my memory now.
Here is what I have come to believe from my experience in the world.

We are all born with gifts, attitudes, ambitions, and innate drives. Their expression, in the wrong context, manipulated or put into hyper-drive, can come across as poor behavior (and it is), they can hurt people, as well as damage relationships and opportunities. But that attitude, ambition, and drive is still a gift, it us just misapplied.

We are all born with gifts, attitudes, ambitions, and innate drives. Their expression, in the wrong context, manipulated or put into hyper-drive, can come across as poor behavior [and it is], they can hurt people, as well as damage relationships and opportunities. But that attitude, ambition, and drive is still a gift, it us just misapplied.

Let me break this down for you and hopefully it will reframe part of your life as well.

In the mall I told my dad, "Everyone here is going to know my name." I came across as selfish and self-centered and that was true. What I did not understand was that deep down, this attitude, ambition, and drive was an expression of something beautiful and pure inside of me. I knew that I was born to not only lead, but to lead and do big things. I believed that the world was not just going to be something that happened to me but that I would happen to the world as well, in a big, impactful, and noticeable way to people around me.

I had misapplied this gift, this attitude, ambition, and drive in a way that came across as selfish and self-centered and that was true - just like my student misapplied his strength, defiance, and stubbornness, but at the bottom of that pile is something remarkable. It's something I value and understand about myself now, it's good that I want to do big things because it is born into me. It's good that my student was able to demonstrate so much strength and immovable force with me as his teacher – it was just applied in the wrong way, expressed in the wrong context; he was just standing up to the wrong person.

I'm curious if there was something about your upbringing, maybe something you would consistently get in trouble for that you had labeled a poor behavior and tried your best to remove – but at the bottom of it, there's something amazing there. Something worth fighting for, protecting, and presenting in its true form.

I could go for one of those breadsticks right now.

CHAPTER 42

In This House We Believe...

Do you remember when there was a mass shooting in Paris in November of 2015? In moments almost everyone on Facebook and Instagram had changed their profile picture to the French flag or an overlay that says, "I stand with Paris." The world seemed to have (digitally) united under a banner against hate and violence.

There's this house I pass when I am on my run in the mornings. There's a sign in the front yard that I've seen many other places. It reads like this...

In this house, we believe:
Love is love
Women's rights are human rights
Black Lives matter
There are great cops
No human being is illegal
Science is real
Kindness is everything
Diversity makes us stronger
Injustice anywhere is a threat to justice everywhere

I'm so surprised they can fit so many words on that tiny sign, I think to myself as I continue my jog. I'm jogging so slow and still seem to be out of air at every step.

Worst. Jogger. Ever.

That's a lot of words on a sign, that's a lot of belief too, they seem to have every belief covered.

I chuckle to myself as I think that the sign should read *"don't cancel us, we believe and support everything."* I am curious if the motive of the sign is to sincerely express support or to stand as a masked defense against the cancel culture that will devour you if you have a contrary opinion, ask a question, or have a dissenting view on an issue they support with their life.

In my head I start running through the phrases on the sign.

Love is love.
Unspoken but an obvious nod to the LGBTQ+ agenda. That's catchy. I love love too. I am in love with my wife and my children. I love my friends. My cousin loves his boyfriend. I love pizza too. The idea of everyone loving each other and being fine with it sounds great! What about a guy who loves two women and would like to marry both? Is love still love? What about the 30-year-old woman in love with a 15-year-old who loves them back? Is love still love? Are you catching where I'm going with this? At what point will you be cancelled for partially objecting, raising concern, or putting some boundaries on "love is love." The phrase looks and sounds good but inevitably seems to contradict itself.

Women's rights are human rights
Yikes. I can already feel readers about to pounce. Take a breath. An unspoken nod to the pro-choice movement. I agree, women's rights are human rights. What if the baby inside of that woman is a woman? Another phrase on that list is "science is real." According to science, a baby has a beating heart and measurable brain waves two weeks after conception. It seems the only difference between referring to this life as a person with rights or a clump of cells is our view on whether or not we actually want to have the baby.

Now, I probably ruffled some of your feathers there. I knew it, you might be thinking, *now I know Joe's politics.* Not in the least.

I am for life and for people wherever I see it. A strong fault of our thinking is that if you are for something you are against the other.

(i.e. if you are for an unborn child, you must be against the mother and her right to choose). I am for the lives of both, actually.

I am also interested in thinking critically about our thought processes. Is it possible to celebrate and support anything and everything without the beliefs contradicting each other?

Believe it or not, this is not even the point of this chapter. I'd like to teach you a term called "performative allyship." This is a very important term for you to understand in today's world.

Remember the initial story I told up above about the shooting in Paris and how everyone changed their profile picture to Stand with Paris? That is a prime example of what performative allyship is. It is positioning yourself, posturing yourself, presenting a picture of yourself to your community and the world – in an effort to convince them of your beliefs and convictions. While simultaneously nothing outside of your profile picture shows that these beliefs express themselves in your daily actions.

My friend, are we connecting dots?

If I believe. It must be expressed outside of my yard sign. If I believe, it must be alive in my life outside of a Facebook status. If I "stand" with a group or cause, my physical body better have stood next to a human being.

Performative allyship, at its root is performance. It is a show in an effort to control the way people see us. Performative allyship is the illusion that nothing about my life has to show I believe what I believe. I can simply just believe.

We cannot play the part without being the person.

If you believe in something, how then can we show it outside of a declaration in our front yard or on our Instagram?

You can show your belief by giving the best of your time, talents, and money.

That's it.

I intentionally try to use "we" language when I talk so I'm going to make a hard pivot for a second.

If the cause, the belief, or the person is not worth the best of your time… if the cause or the belief or the person is not worth you applying your talents to move it forward… if you would like other people to give the money toward this belief, this person, or this cause, yet you are unwilling to give the best of your own money toward it: You don't believe in it, you are performing.

> If the cause, the belief, or the person is not worth the best of your time… if the cause or the belief or the person is not worth you applying your talents to move it forward… if you would like other people to give the money toward this belief, this person, or this cause, yet you are unwilling to give the best of your own money toward it: You don't believe in it, you are performing.

Performative allyship will allow you to blend in and possibly keep you from being canceled. It will 100% keep you from living. Let the world feel the weight of who you are and let them deal with it.

CHAPTER 43

"Now My Thoughts Pay For Meals I Never Had As A Kid" (And The Art Of Celebration)

I vividly remember sitting in the drive though of Hot-and-Now with my parents when I was young and choosing between two hamburgers or one cheeseburger. It was a tough choice, especially because I knew that I was going to have to end up splitting my fries with my little brother, too. I usually picked the two hamburgers because it was more food; it may have been the off-brand McDonald's, but it was still special to get takeout. I really liked the water there as well (would not dream of asking for a pop), it was cold and it was city water – the city water was so crisp and delicious. We lived in the country and drank well water, which was fine as well, but I did enjoy the city water with ice. I would pop the bubbles on the tops of the cups that said "Diet" and "Coke" knowing one day I'd go through a drive-through and order a pop. We didn't go to McDonald's, too expensive. Happy meals were not part of my upbringing unless I was with grandma and grandpa and that was really special.

McDonald's came out with a dollar menu when I was around 12 and we started going to McDonalds; we could order two things off the menu and I loved being at McDonald's. I would still eye the combos on the board from the seat, the crispy chicken sandwich combo that came with a large fry and a drink, gosh that looked so good.

In 5th grade I was riding in the car with a friend Reed and his mom. I was going to go on a trip with his family for the weekend up north and before leaving town we went through the drive through at McDonald's. When we pulled up to order at the drive-through window, I was curious how Reed and his mom ordered.

Were they dollar menu people?

"Can I have a 12 -piece chicken nugget meal with Coke, a Big Mac meal with Sprite and..(she looked back at me) Joey?"

"Crispy chicken sandwich meal, please" I said to her only semi-confident and thinking to myself *I can't believe I am getting a whole meal off the menu.* She continued to look at me and I almost apologized thinking I had over-ordered, I almost said "Never mind, just two hamburgers!"

"What do you want to drink, Joe?"

"Oh, Sprite!" I said still a little confused that this felt so foreign to me.

It was the best McDonalds' meal I ever had. It tasted so good. I got my own bag, my own medium fry, tall Sprite, and a chicken sandwich that came in a box. Wow, it was wonderful.

I recently recorded a song with Tae Sosa where I say the line "now my thoughts pay for meals I never had as a kid." When The Lion Heart Crew and I go through the drive through of McDonald's, everyone gets a numbered meal, a pop, their own fry, and I pay for it. When we go out to eat in the evening after we have put in solid hours of work doing performances during the day, I believe we have something to celebrate. Our group is doing pivotal and important work around the country. Each day we hear stories of students who were considering ending their lives and something about the paint on the canvas, the ending of the story, or Tae's lyrics has stopped

When The Lion Heart Crew and I go through the drive through of McDonald's, everyone gets a numbered meal, a pop, their own fry, and I pay for it. When we go out to eat in the evening after we have put in solid hours of work doing performances during the day, I believe we have something to celebrate.

them and moved them in a new and life-giving direction.

Because of this, we flex the muscle of celebration in The Lion Heart Experience. It is a value of our group, to celebrate and stamp special moments. To lift a glass to the day, to each other. We celebrate. We order drinks, appetizers, the fifty-dollar steak, and usually a dessert – and I pay for it.

The Lion Heart Experience began, is sustained, and flourishes through my thoughts expressed and brought to life. My friendships, connections, and networks flowing along the stream of belief, grit, and talent. An idea of a performance where story would be fused with visual art, music, and deep human connection that started in a little Detroit school is now one of the premiere suicide-prevention programs in the country.

I will take a number 3, medium with Coke, please.

CHAPTER 44

Finding Your Voice

When I was 16, I loved singing John Mayer songs as I was learning to use my voice and my talents performing with my guitar on street corners. His song "Waiting On The World to Change," was always a classic to pull out while I sat leaning against a light post on the concrete.

"Me and all my friends, we're all misunderstood.
They say we stand for nothing and there's no way we ever could.
We see everything that's going wrong, with the world and those who lead it.
We just feel like we don't have the means
To rise above and beat it.

So, we keep waiting, waiting on the world to change."

I strained my voice to achieve the scratchy tone that John Mayer delivered all his songs with. My voice felt so plain and vanilla. Sometimes I would strain my voice early on in the day so that when I sang it sounded naturally scratchy and smokey. I wanted to sound like John.

When I first began speaking, I would listen to other public speakers and grab their cadences and tone, I loved their delivery and their conviction. I wanted to have the conviction and energy of Steven Furtick when I spoke and the depth of Rich Nathan, both speakers I looked up to.

Before long, on stage speaking and on street corners singing - I started to realize the only thing missing was...me. I was a hodge-podge sparkly combination of vocal timbre, delivery, and content that landed me singing trying to sound like someone else and speaking trying to speak like someone else. It was enough to land some attention and achievement but not enough to satisfy me on the inside because I knew I was not being myself.

This was before YouTube and Tik Tok too. My exposure to content and people was limited, at least by today's standards.

I was playing the part without being the person, my inner-world had the feeling equivalent to eating too much cake. Lacking substance.

> I was playing the part without being the person, my inner world had the feeling equivalent to eating too much cake. Lacking substance and depth.

It took a long time, and most importantly a lot of time **not** listening to my favorite musicians and speakers, to find my own voice, my own stories, my own delivery, my own personality, my own vocal style, my own passion. At the time I'm writing this, I'm 35 years old and feel like I am just arriving at the early stages of living as a genuine version of me.

Maybe you can relate. How much of you is really *you* right now? How much of who you are, how you operate, what you are passionate about, what you stand for is *you* and how much of It is seeing someone on YouTube, Instagram or Tik Tok and adopting what they do, or even how they think, how the talk or joke. How much of your world view, your style, your sexuality, your view of friendship or commitment has been formed by your personal development or by what looks good and is trendy on social media?

This is tough to digest, isn't it?

Let me try this from another angle. The world needs you. It needs the biggest, fullest, most beautiful expression of who you are. It needs you and your unique voice, style, quirks, and expressions - just like it needs me and my voice. I don't want to offer the world a hodgepodge version of myself; a little bit of me and a whole lot of me trying to be someone and something else. Like a cake with too much frosting. I don't want to sit on a street corner singing someone else's song even trying to sound like them. I don't want to give a message someone else delivered with belief because it was their message to give.

Sometimes the key to being you isn't adding layers, it's taking away.

Maybe a good action step for you might be to take a step away from the heavy influences on your screen and in your ears. Take some time to figure out who you are and learn to delight in it. You can't love yourself any more than you know yourself.

Believe this though, friend, I'm on the other side of this book standing and cheering you on because someday, I hope the real version of me gets to meet the most real and authentic version of you.

CHAPTER 45

Bead Necklaces, Mardi-Gras, Steak, and Shrimp

I sat my trombone case down on the floor and plopped down in the band room of my high school. I loved this room, so much so that my friend Jeff and I learned how to sneak into it. The band room was my home - all my favorite people were here, my favorite moments, my favorite teacher. Sometimes I would slide my debit card across the top of the door at lunch time (unlocking the door) just to be in this room.

Today was going to be life changing for 15-year-old me, I just didn't know it yet. I sat in a semi-circle of some of the best musicians in the school, probably 8 of us all together. Todd and James were there, I couldn't believe how good they were at the trumpet. Brian was there, a senior percussionist that could play anything. Nick, Art, Allen... This was the A team, then there was me. I was pretty good, but I still had that lingering feeling that this room was over my head in talent. What were we even doing here today? Our music teacher, Mr. Smokovitz (we called him Smoke) just asked us if we were free this evening and if we had some time to sneak out of our last hour class.

Smoke is a pretty unassuming guy, shorter and stocky, mustache, salt and pepper hair. His office is a complete mess, broken instruments, music pages, awards, trophies, and music scores on his desk. Most of the time he blends into the mess, and you have to look carefully to see if he is in his office. Yet I'm equally intrigued and eager around him because this man has facilitated the classroom that has become home for me. I love this room, I love the people in it, I trust whatever happens in this room. I love Smoke for who he is and whatever we are doing today, I'm here for it.

We all pull our instruments out and Smoke walks out of his office with some music books most of had not seen since 6th grade. We chuckle at the nostalgia and flip through the pages – recalling memories of middle school and some of the specific tunes in this book called essential elements that still rang in our ears. Yet, we are still mildly confused as to why he is setting this elementary book in front of us in high school.

Smoke clears his throat and grabs his trumpet from a stand next to his podium in the center of our semicircle. He blows warm air through the mouthpiece and bounces his fingers over the valves to release the air through the metals and pathways of the twisted silver metals.

"Find When The Saints Go Marching In on page 37, please."

He motions to us to lift our instruments as he counts us off and we play a familiar melody, watered down to the most basic, most vanilla version that took us all back to learning the instruments that Smoke taught us in 6th grade.

"Take a look at those notes on the page for a minute, get that melody in your mind, your fingers and your arms – so that you don't have to look at it anymore."

We all took a few minutes to play with the notes on the page and engrain them and the melody into our minds.

"We are going to build out a Mardi Gras, New-Orleans style version of this. That basic melody is just our starting place," Smoke said.

Note to the reader:
If you are not familiar - A Mardi Gras, New-Orleans style band would be something like from The Princess And The Frog. The iconic Disney movie set in the southern Bayou. A small roaming band creating celebration in the streets of New Orleans with a

signature swinging rhythm tugging and pulling on each note –
taking familiar melodies like When The Saints Go Marching In – and
making even the most reserved bystander want to grab someone
and swing them around.

Magic happened over the next 10 minutes as Smoke demonstrated
how to take our unique melody and infuse it with a southern style
and interpretation. He transformed that little melody from our 6th
grade book into a real-life Mardi-Gras band. He turned the band
room (once again) into this oasis and invigorating environment of
creativity.

"Ok." Looking at his watch, "Head back to class and I'll meet you at
Bennigan's at 6:30 tonight." and he walked away.

Bennigan's, in Midland Michigan where I was from, was one of our
favorite restaurants. It was a chain, but since most of us didn't
travel much, we didn't know that. We just knew it was an awesome
spot to eat. We all packed up, looking at each other with shrugs
and eyes that simply communicated that we were up for whatever
Smoke had for us at 6:30.

Later that evening, when we arrived at Bennigan's with our
instruments, Smoke told us that from 6:30-8:00 we would be
wandering the restaurant with our newly revised and revamped
When The Saints Go Marching In tune. He gave us beads we draped
around our necks in celebration of Mardi Gras and we began
assembling our instruments.

A live restaurant band.

How in the world did we pull this off and how did it sound so good
and so fitting?

As we meandered around the restaurant, the song would morph
and customize itself leaving room for solos and breaks. At times
our instruments stopped and we just sang our parts. Eight rag-
tag musicians, our teacher and me (who this entire time) is still
wondering how I made it into such an amazing experience.

The night was coming to a performative close and we sat down at
a table near the bar. Our waitress came out from the back of the

kitchen and asked us if she could get us started with anything to drink and some appetizers for the table. My eyebrows raised.

Anything? A drink and an appetizer? Who's paying for this? I thought to myself.

Mid-thought I said, "I'd love a Coca-Cola and the chicken wings appetizer." Smoke looked at me with a small head nod and a grin.

"How about your main entrée?" the waitress said as she came back around the table and looked at me "You can order anything off the menu, it's on us tonight," putting her hand on her chest motioning that the restaurant was taking care of the check.

I ordered the steak and shrimp, a meal that was off limits for a person that was part of a nine-member family. With six siblings, we could not run up a bill like that, so it was water, no apps, and your entrée better be under $17.

This was one of the best meals of my life. I wish I still had a bead necklace from the night to remember it by.

This was one of the first nights that I saw a talent morph into a meal. Smoke knew this, I was just introduced to the feeling, and I was hooked. I can create value? Feel alive and passionate and it can translate into beautiful meals and memories?

I had a so much fun with my friends, being creative and free while at the same time the restaurant we were at benefitted from our talents and atmosphere we created.

I am forever chasing this feeling, my friends. Perhaps some of you are about to join me. You may hear me refer to this as *Chasing The Bucket.*

Part of the underlying current of The Lion Heart Experience is the thought that maybe, I could do something with my life that other people find value and worth in experiencing – while at the same time I experience the freedom and creativity of being who I am built to be. Alive and passionate with my favorite people, in my favorite spaces, with my favorite foods. It's out there, I've tasted it. It started with a beat-up trombone and chilling at Bennigan's with my friends and Smoke.

When I meet people like Tae and Jeremiah, Olivia and Julie, all members of The Lion Heart Crew - I can't help but step into Smoke's shoes and say, "Follow me." I know how to morph your talent into a meal. There's a life over here.

Every time I hear *When The Saints Go Marching In*, I'm reminded that an amazing meal and more amazing memories could be near. I'm ready to grab whatever I need and follow Smoke.

CHAPTER 46

What is That Blah Feeling?

I can't get moving. I feel like I've tried everything, and I just feel like I'm emotionally standing in mud. I have things to do but my motivation seems to be in negative numbers. I'm not depressed or anxious – I'm something else. I feel like I'm on the threshold of both productivity and wanting to curl up in a ball. I'm Just Blah. Not moving forward or backward just not in motion in my mind or body.

Do you know this feeling? There's a word for it, I only learned it less than a year ago. This feeling is called *languishing*. It's when you are neither up nor down, you are not un-productive, but you are not killing it either, you are ok, but it wouldn't take much to send you into the "not" ok category. Instead of standing you might lay on the floor, tucking your arms under your body and surprise yourself with how comfortable the carpet is on your face.

Why is understanding this word important? It is not to pull yourself out of it or be satisfied living with the feeling each day – when we understand an emotion, it gives us a small sense of power over it. Naming the emotion offers you a touch of authority because now you have a name. Lori, one of our amazing team members with Lion Heart says "name the beast."

I'm languishing today.

When you recognize emotions, you are able to extend something really wonderful to yourself; compassion. Self-compassion is the highest form of compassion. For me personally, it's easier for me to be compassionate and understanding to others than to myself. Try saying these things to yourself out loud:

> When you recognize emotions, you are able to extend something really wonderful to yourself, compassion. Self-compassion is the highest form of compassion.

"It's ok, there's no rush."

"Everybody feels this way sometimes, today might be my day, that's alright."

"Today I am languishing, it's not the feeling I wanted for the day, but it is what is happening in my body, I'm going to take a walk after I get up from this carpet."

Languishing is not depression, it's just part of the rhythms of life and our bodies and it's ok - you are neither a mess nor perfectly put together either. On days I am languishing, I find it very difficult to work, focus, and be productive. I try my best to jumpstart my body with a walk, a healthy meal, and some breathing exercises. If that doesn't work, I ask myself what I can adjust today to accommodate this new raincloud in my mind. Can I do the work tomorrow I was planning to do today? Maybe I could replace that time with a nap?

It won't always work out that you can offer yourself a full day off when you are languishing - but your body and your mind will love you for offering it some compassion.

CHAPTER 47

A Liminal Space

Let's get back to therapy with Jackson. I'm sitting on my usual loveseat, my feet are draped over the arms and I'm looking out the window at the people making their way to the stores down below. I wonder if they look up and see me if they know I'm trying to sort out my life and my emotions with a professional. *I could go for a latte at that coffee shop over there,* I thought to myself.

"Let's talk about your work, Joe," Jackson interrupts my observations with a question.

In my sessions with him I had been talking with him about transitioning from my classroom to possibly doing The Lion Heart Experience full-time. Teaching in Detroit had left me feeling all types of messed up. I loved what I was doing in my classroom. I also could not get over the fact that I knew, I knew that kids at this school were not being set up for success. There are just too many monstrous issues in Detroit education. Bad facilities, no opportunities, over half of the teachers at my school were not even certified teachers, there was no library or playground. Kids that can't read just get passed to the next grade, there's no special education. I felt like I was playing a part in upholding a broken system. I needed to be done. The thought of following through with that decision felt daunting and I couldn't bear the thought of leaving my students behind. We sat and processed my desire to discontinue leading the non-profit in the city that I had started 8 years ago, as well. I was afraid of letting people down or being seen as a failure to people around me. A couple weeks prior, my wife Heather and I had moved from the suburbs to the city of Detroit with Eli and Selah, we had our third child Amelie a few weeks before and I was recovering from a major surgery from a life-threatening blood-clot complication.

Maybe the people down below walking around in the parking lot could see what I mess I was. Was this glass tinted?

"You are in a liminal space," Jackson said softly to me. I refocused back on the conversation - everything he has shared with me and that I have learned about myself has drastically shifted my life.

"What is a liminal space?" I asked him.

"Well, in architecture a liminal space would be a hallway or a staircase. It's not your resting place, it's meant to move you to the next location. It's a transitional space. Liminal."

He continued, "Liminal spaces exist in nature too." A crab will leave its shell in search for a new and more spacious shell during its life. How do you think the crab might feel as it sheds its shell and moves in search of the new one?"

"Vulnerable? Small? Maybe afraid?" I said, imagining this little naked crab wandering through the ocean floor without a shell. I could only picture the crab from *the Little Mermaid* and I don't think that's the one he was trying to get me to think about. I don't even know what a shell-less crab looks like.

"You are in a time of transition, Joe. A liminal space with your occupation, in search of a new shell, new rhythms with family and marriage and home, the stairs and hallways of life - your body healing and reminding you of its fragility."

A liminal space can be a day, it can be a month, it can be a season or a year, but it still is what it is - liminal, transitional, not a final destination.

A liminal space can be a day, it can be a month, it can be a season or a year, but it still is what it is — liminal, transitional, not a final destination.

Some of you reading this are in a liminal space in your relationships, your understanding of yourself. You are in a transitional time of your life with your body as it matures. Maybe you live somewhere new - there's transition happening, and you are beating yourself up because you feel like you should be good by now, you've had enough time or you should have it figured out. But it's a liminal space and when you finally have a name for it you can extend yourself some grace, some understanding and compassion - it feels so good.

How's the ocean going for you?

CHAPTER 48

Pearls, Pigs, Matches, and Ashes

Let's stay in therapy for a few minutes. I am thinking to myself that I have never told you what Jackson looks like - I'd like to help complete your mental picture so you can best see the conversations that him and I had.

Jackson is about 6 feet tall, but most of the time he is sitting so my (experienced) perception of his height is about 4 feet tall sitting straight up. He always wears short sleeve button ups; they are very fitting because I think he does cross-fit or something - I haven't asked him. I'm never quite sure how far I can pry into his life as he is helping me do surgery on mine. His arms have a few tattoos on them that, in my head, must be very meaningful because he is a therapist. He's fit, he's slender but muscular with a tight haircut - short on the sides a little longer at the top and his hair is blondish reddish. He has glasses (as all therapists should) so he can look at me curiously over the top of the rims as he writes on his clipboard. *I wonder what he's writing, did I just say something very good or very bad,* I think to myself. *I have got to be the most messed up, selfish person who has ever sat in this room.*

His glasses are tortoise brown colored, bold frame. He's got a great jawline, (I say that in the most plutonic way) but it's the type of jawline you don't cover up with a beard, so his face is clean shaven. He wears nice dress shoes with ankle socks so you can see the top of his ankles near his heels. I can tell he is into the latest fashion even though If I asked him, he probably would say his wife just buys his clothes.

Jackson's eyes are warm and inviting. Disarming and genuine and I love eyes like that. They make me feel comfortable. When he smiles you know it is real, same with his laugh or moments of exclamation where he identifies with something I say and his eyes get big and he says "Yea I get that!" I really like when he shares stories with me about his own little kids because I know we both have toddlers at home and if he's anything like me, we are equally proud of our parenting and equally scared to death that we are just messing up our kids.

When Jackson says "I'm proud of you" to me, I feel it. He doesn't say it jokingly, or lightly. He doesn't raise his vocal tone or change the timbre of his voice. He knows I take my inner-world, my thoughts, the patterns of my life, and my experienced emotions seriously and I work on all the things we talk about in our sessions after I leave in real life.

He tells me he's proud of me when I come back and report to him about how I exercised restraint in areas of my life I usually could not control like my internal anger or stories I tell myself about the world and people around me. Or when I stop myself from panicking with increased perspective and awareness in a situation where I would look normal on the outside and be frantic on the inside. Or when I give myself compassion.

He knows that I grew up a pastor's kid so I'm familiar with a story of Jesus getting baptized when he's an adult. He pulls out this story to use with me as a launch-pad for conversation. In the story Jesus comes up out of the water after being baptized and everyone hears God's voice boom from the skies. "This is my son, who brings me great joy." End of speech.

"That was it Joe," Jackson said while he recounted this story for me. It was not in anything that Jesus had done, accomplished, or worked for that God said *This my boy, I'm proud of him.* It's just that he was his boy.

This story meant a lot to my heart because accomplishment drives me. Even when I'm doing good things I want to excel, be renown, competitive. In a way I can tell that I sometimes feel like I need to earn something or prove something to the world around me.

That's why I'm sitting here in Jackson's office on the same day that I received the Teacher of The Year Award for the city of Detroit. Something wasn't adding up because although my outside world seemed to be in order and was notable, my inside world was a wreck.

In my song "Most of us" there's a line that says:

Sitting all alone, laying on my couch and can't breathe
Laying in bed conversations in my head, won't stop, can't sleep
Zero to a hundred I can never get above it always gets the best of me
Now who gets the best of me?

Maybe I'm late
I think about it all lately
"I'm fine, its straight"
Not the one that needs saving
Most of us we cry alone
Just wanna somehow make it home

In this song I recall the times I look relaxed, and my heart is racing. I can't stop the flood of thoughts through my brain - most of them anxious or angry at others. My emotions (although mostly unseen) go from non-existent to what feels like raging. My anger at something doesn't express itself with me punching a wall, I just feel like my soul is foaming at the mouth.

While I write this, I just re-read that last line and the word picture feels uncomfortable to think about but it's how it felt - maybe there's a young person reading this who is in the same spot.

That's why when Jackson says "I'm proud of you," I feel soothed - because I feel like I have had to earn that, work for it, grind for it for a long time everywhere else, but it sounds and feels different when he says it because I can tell Jackson is tapping into the type of pride that God was expressing about his son, Jesus.

I'm proud of him just because he's my boy, that's it.

So where do the pearls and pigs come in? That's the name of this little chapter.

(breathe)

"I'm the angriest at the people I help the most, the people I love and want to see succeed. I give the best of my time, my energy, and my resources on their behalf. Why do I love them so much and am so angry at them too because I feel like they don't appreciate it?" I say to Jackson.

He looks at me with compassionate eyes, knowing that it is the truth that I do love to help people, I do the work to put them in a place of privilege, I genuinely love to extend myself on their behalf. He can see that it bothers me, deeply, to not feel appreciated.

At this time, I'm leading a non-profit in the city of Detroit whose sole purpose is to come alongside the marginalized and disenfranchised - helping to put teens and families on different paths, increase opportunity - while at the same time, these have become the people I resent the most because I see little to no actual action on their part to change their circumstances. It makes me want to throw up my middle finger and walk away.

Both middle fingers, actually.

The leaders I work with in the non-profit often tell me they can't show up because (helping others) doesn't work in their schedule.

…

"Well, we can't change anyone outside this room, Joe" Jackson says to me taking a breath that shows me we have a lot of work to do - I'm ready for it though - I do not want to feel this way.

Through thoughtful conversation and questions over days, Jackson brought me to some important realizations about myself.

1. **I struggle with entitlement**
    Man, this threw me for a loop because entitlement bothers me so much. Like when I pay for someone's meal and they don't even say thank you - it makes me feel like they are thinking that

I was supposed to pay for their meal, or that they *deserved* a free meal. Just say thank you, Jerk. What's wrong with you?

Jackson: "You struggle with entitlement because even in generosity you expect a thank you and it bothers you to your core when you don't receive it. You feel you are entitled to their gratitude, yes?"

I take a deep breathe. And another. Equally bummed and equally relieved that there's something to fix inside of me.

2. **"Do you have any friends that you are not in charge of developing?"**
   This was a question that Jackson asked me. "Do you have anyone that you just enjoy being around because you love being around them? A friend. Not someone you are helping or mentoring or employing or leading, just a friend whose company you enjoy?"

   I can count on one hand the people in my life that fit that category, and it's basically just my wife Heather. No real friends. Just mentees, or people I would meet with to cultivate. I feel embarrassed writing that. I would spend the next year cultivating a couple of these friendships that I enjoy today.

3. **"The people you are helping, did they ask for your help?"**
   Yikes! I can feel myself tense up when he asks me that question because it pokes at a complex that I have tried, with everything inside of me to avoid, especially being a white guy in a mostly black and brown context and being a teacher in inner-city Detroit: A savior complex.

   So far, I've been pretty chill in our sessions, but I do not want to get labeled with a savior complex. I sit up and put my feet on the ground, they are no longer draped over the arm of the chair. I'm wanting to push against this.

   Jackson notices my physical reaction to this. I know he is not against me – but I pride myself on being a good helper. If I lose this or realize that I have been hurting instead of helping – I'm going to lose it.

"A part of this savior dynamic is not so much about how you view other people, Joe." Jackson presses in gently.

This puts me a little at ease because I honestly believe that I am not the answer to all the world's problems, truly.

Jackson: **"If you sense the smallest need, if you even get a small sense that someone needs something - you cannot stop yourself from hopping in and helping, would you say that's true?"**

He says this and it settles into my soul like a tea bag when you place it in a cup of hot water. You start to see the flavor and the color seep out of the bag of spices and leaves into the clear cup. Part of who I am is released, understood, and finally brought out into the open.

(Another deep breath)
Therapy is so good for you but sometimes it feels like working with a trainer at the gym - it will leave you sore and breathless. Yet at the same time, I walk out with a little more understanding of how I'm wired so I can begin to detangle some of the knots in my mind and my heart. I gain perspective on my life. I'm able to extend myself compassion and the cup of tea fills with flavor and color instead of being contained in the tea bag.

What Jackson said is true. It is hard for me to hear or see a need, especially with someone close to me, and to not address it or offer to ease the burden of their (perceived) struggle.

4. **"Are you throwing your pearls to pigs?"**
   Before I unpack this. As you read this, it's important for you to know that when Jackson brought up this phrase he was not calling the people that I help pigs. Therapy is about you; my therapy sessions are about me, not anyone else outside of the room. That is very important for you to remember as I lay this out.

   I have a strong tendency to offer the best of who I am (my

pearls) – my kindness, my generosity, my skills, my friendship, my warmth, and my resources to people who have not asked for them. Those dynamics of my personality are part of what make me a wonderful person. On the flipside, I struggle with the self-control of giving them, over and over, to people that have not asked for them or expressed interest in their value.

If I am not careful - I will have no *pearls* left to give when someone actually needs something or genuinely wants the benefit of my friendship and kinship because I will have wasted them. If I am not careful, as I was now realizing, I will waste the best of who I am on people who, at the end of the day, have not asked for me to add value, fix a problem, or ease a burden.

This brought illumination to the issue I talked about earlier with why I was beginning to resent the people I loved and helped. They didn't ask for my help; I just saw what I considered a need and tried to meet it. Good intentions. Bad results. Very bad results, most of them inside of me.

Matches and Ashes.

Realizing this about myself has allowed me to re-evaluate relational connections in my life. I have let some friendships go; I've released them - which I did not even know was ever an option - because they were one sided. I've narrowed in on relationships and connections that bring me life and do not trigger my need to prove myself or fix a problem that I see.

When it comes to the pearls of who I am, I am the type of person that needs to experience something tangible, something that I feel and see and smell to have a reality settle in. So just last night I did something ceremonial. You might consider something like this if this is ringing true at all for you as well.

I wrote a note about a person that I love and believe in. They have amazing talent and potential – I want with everything inside of me to see them succeed. I often apply the best of my time, talents, and money to help them along in life - then I am angry inside my heart when I feel like they don't appreciate the help, take it for granted, don't even say thank you, or do not pursue opportunity themselves.

Here was my note:

"I am releasing my compulsive and reckless belief in (their name here) that results, inevitably, in frustration, tension, and disappointment from all angles. I've given the best of my time, my efforts, and resources and they have not asked for my help. I can love them and believe in them AND create some emotional distance, boundaries, and space for a better version of myself."

Then I lit the piece of paper on fire and watched in burn and turn to ashes on a cookie sheet in my living room. It was my way of releasing the thought, seeing it change form.

I read this note to my wife, Heather, who has seen me work and extend myself tirelessly for this person. We toasted our wine glasses together. I know myself more now, and when you know yourself more, you can love yourself more.

To the pearls, cheers.

CHAPTER 49

Rerouting

In 700 ft turn left on Lincoln
Rerouting
Turn left to merge onto Stephenson Highway North
In 500 ft, 400 ft, 300 ft, 200 ft, 100 ft
Rerouting
Make a U-Turn now to get back onto the highway
Rerouting.

According to my Apple Maps, I was completely lost this morning. I missed every single turn, every direction, and all suggestions to fix my navigation mistakes.

On this early winter morning, I was taking the Lion Heart Yukon to the dealership about 25 minutes from my house to get some work done on it. In metro-Detroit, there's construction everywhere and it happened to be rush hour, as well. Everyone was headed to the city for work and the highway was packed.

I decided to take backstreets to get to the dealership knowing that it was going to end up taking less time and it would be a much less frustrating drive, avoiding the construction and highway traffic.

The ride was going very well, except I had the dealership locked in as my destination on my phone and Apple Maps did not like the way I was taking to get there.

Siri (with her pure unchanging conviction) kept instructing me "Turn around, rerouting, make a U-turn, rerouting."

I didn't change my course.

"In 200 ft TURN. LEFT"

In her last-ditch attempts to safely deliver me to the Chevrolet Dealer, Siri recommended I shift my path back to the Highway. By this time, I was only a few minutes from my destination, yet Apple Maps could not conceive of the path I was taking to get there.

Reader, I'm curious if you can relate to this story. Some of you may be able to relate on a multitude of levels.

You know where you are going, you know where you are meant to be, you do have a plan, you are aware of what's happening around you, you have considered other opportunities, paths and routes, yet you are bombarded with the constant urges from people close to you to reroute, turn around, make a U-turn and choose another path. You may even be feeling this pressure from yourself.

Good news, I arrived at the dealership, and you will as well.

If you are reading this and you know who you are meant to be, where you are meant to go, and what you are designed to be doing in life – I trust your driving.

I Just Knew

In 2017, it had been about two years of me balancing teaching full time and taking my vacation days to travel to other schools with The Lion Heart Crew to perform in other schools in the Midwest. Our name was getting passed around to some amazing schools. More and more opportunities seemed to come our way – it appears that being reminded of your worth is a market with an infinite need and we happen to be amazing at it. It also turns out that students leaving school to travel with a teacher around the country did not vibe well with the teacher handbook! Nevertheless, this always felt like it was written for me.

In the early days of Lion Heart, the crew and I relied on host homes in cities and states that we had not been to before. We made some beautiful relationships that we still lean into to this day with families that have hosted us and took a chance on our motley crew and story. We traveled in a minivan weighed down so low by our trailer that the tires skimmed the wheelbase, heating the back of the van with friction to the point that riders in the back like Tae would start sweating. It was McDonalds and Wendy's on the road. Low budget. The first Lion Heart performances we traveled to were $450 because I had no idea how much schools would be willing to pay for us to come. Every school that paid barely covered the cost of gas, meals, and sound equipment.

I remember the first night that we got put up in a hotel. A

conference we were going to perform at in the capitol of Michigan got all of us hotel rooms. The hotel had a pool, I still remember that swim. They also paid for our meal at the restaurant in the hotel. I had used my last vacation day to be at this conference with the Lion Heart Crew.

I remember lying in bed at the hotel wondering if this could ever be a real part of our lives. People putting us up in hotels, paying for our meals, could we make a living doing this?

Search up "The Lion Heart Experience Capitol Tour" to see us in this phase of life on YouTube.

I finished that year teaching, completing my 9th year teaching in Detroit and returned at the end of the summer for professional development. My classroom was all set up with the same sound system we traveled with for Lion Heart. The recording microphone that the early Lion Heart songs were recorded sat mounted next to my desk. Eight-foot posters of Lion Heart Crew members draped over my wall like NBA players – great things happened in this room. I walked into our morning session and the dean of students began our training on the new software we would be using for grading this year. My colleagues all opened their laptops to sign in and take notes.

I sat still and my heart began to race.

No one but me was able to feel the fog, disconnection, and displacement that filled my body. It was unmistakable. I was done teaching. I wasn't meant to be here anymore – the chapter closed.

No one but me was able to feel the fog, disconnection, and displacement that filled my body. It was unmistakable. I was done teaching. I wasn't meant to be here anymore — the chapter closed.

I walked out of the room to my classroom and tugged on the posters that hung on my wall. Knowing that once I rip these posters down there is no going back for me internally. I just knew it was over.

By the end of that day, I had sat down with my principal and superintendent to let them know that I was done. Tae, Arthur, and Keon (all early members of The Lion Heart Crew) all showed up to move nine years of teaching into the Lion Heart Trailer and I walked out of the classroom for the last time.

I just knew it was over and I could not stay. I decided to bet on myself.

I share this story because some of you are still in a chapter that has closed. You know it's over. This small whisper telling you that there's a new chapter for you has been suffocated with expectation, fear, and obligation.

What are you supposed to be doing right now?

CHAPTER 51

Green Lights and The Truth

I am the oldest of seven kids and we had two family vehicles. One was a white, 12-passenger van with the license plate "MNYKIDZ" that my mom usually drove - my dad also drove a white Jeep Wrangler. It was a stick shift, which I hated him for making me learn how to drive because it's so embarrassing to stall your car in an intersection for not popping the clutch right or the lurching forward when you shift wrong. Honestly, I love it now because I'm good at it, but it took a while.

I took drivers education my sophomore year and was really excited to finally be able to get my license.

I had a near-death experience with my dad when I first had my permit. I was driving my dad's Jeep and he was in the passenger seat. We needed to turn left at an intersection with two lanes of traffic on each side and the light was green. Casually, while the light was green, I turned the wheel to make my left turn and was deathly surprised that oncoming traffic was not stopping. Horns blared, wheels skidded, my dad's hands pressed against the side window and front dash of the jeep.

"Joe! Are you trying to kill us?! What are you doing?! Go! Go! Get out of here, we're going to die!"

Indignant, I shouted back "I had the right of way! The light was green! I had the right of way!”

“No! No, you didn’t have the right of way!” My dad shouted back in the near-death tone while the moment was still flushed with adrenaline.

“The light was green, Dad, I *HAD* the right of way” I said firmly, profoundly convinced, excusing myself from nearly killing my dad and me.
My dad, still breathing heavily, now, with a touch of annoyance and anger answered me again “Joe, when you are turning left into oncoming traffic, you do NOT have the right of way. That is the truth. I don’t care how firmly you believe otherwise. The green light means you can go *AFTER* oncoming traffic has cleared. You can say *‘I had the right of way, I had the right of way’* all you want, but you almost killed us.”

Truthfully, I did almost kill my dad and I turning into oncoming traffic that day. It didn’t matter if I believed I had the right of way. The truth is that a maneuver like that - ends lives. That’s it.

It’s a real and silly story that happened one time, yet I see this story every day in different contexts.

We live in a world where you are encouraged to live your truth, find your truth, speak your truth, be your truth - *your* truth doesn’t have to be *my* truth, you must accept everyone’s truths unless you want to be cancelled. Affirm and embrace. If you believe it, it’s your truth.

My young friends reading this, may I challenge your thinking in a post-truth culture?

Perhaps there is truth, a standard for living, perhaps there are bounds to stay within or accountability that will inevitably happen for our lives – perhaps, just like me turning my dad’s Jeep into oncoming traffic, it will not matter how deeply, or firmly you believe something if it is not, in-fact, the truth.

The truth was going to crash into the front of my dad's car with me in the driver's seat regardless of my indignant, unflinching belief in my right of way under that green light.

I wonder if our all-accepting truth culture is really just a subconscious way we want to avoid having to submit ourselves to a standard, expectation or authority. So, we create our own truths about friendship, relationships, marriage, sex, money and we encourage others to find their own truths as well.

Now, I can feel a few of you seething through the pages. Your strong independent personality pulses through the pages back to me.

I knew it, he's about to push his religious views on us.

Not in the least, my friends. Take a breath.

I am here to stimulate your thoughts and challenge you. The back of this book says you may meet a deeper, more self-aware, and more developed version of you at the end of this book. We are in that process, together.

Our "live your truth" culture has left us with some staggering realities to face when it comes to our overall health (Heart, Soul, Mind, Strength).

> *"We're not scared to die, we're all scared to stick around."*
> *– Glow, The Lion Heart Experience.*

The American Psychological Association reports that more than 20% of teens have considered suicide. The article continues:

"A report from the Centers for Disease Control and Prevention (CDC) looking at mental health and suicidal behaviors from 2011 to 2021 indicates that 13% of high school girls had attempted suicide (30% had seriously considered it). That jumped to more than 20% for LGBTQ+ teens"

When I consider that we are amid the freest, most expressive, most inclusive, most affirming culture in the world where you can be what you want, say what you want, post what you want, identify as what you want – you can speak your truth, live your truth, create your truth, find your truth – shouldn't we be seeing the quality of our collective mental health rise? Shouldn't we want to live?

We can finally be who we are, no bounds, I do not have to live under your oppressive truth that limits my personal freedom and expression, nor you under mine.

So, why do so many people want to end their lives?
Have I lost you in the deep end or are you still with me? I'd like to use an example that will be relatable to everyone reading his.

Sex.

Oh, shoot. Yes...sex.

Is there a truth about sex or is it all up to us to figure out and explore and live our truth? I'd like to lay it all out on the table.

The formation of a sexual identity

I remember one of our most memorable Lion Heart rides to another state where we asked each other if we ever got "the talk" from our parents. "The talk" being a breakdown of what sex was and at what age that talk did or did not happen. It's actually a really interesting conversation to have if you want to kick it around. We all had different experiences, some of us had the most uncomfortable sit-down with our parents EVER. Some of us just got handed a condom and were told to be careful. Some of us discovered an older sibling or cousin watching pornography and that was the earliest introduction to sex - but all of us had a sexual identity that was being formed from a young age.

You can correct me with I'm wrong, but our culture is hyper-sexual and is represented in our artforms (music, TV shows, movies), encouraging sexual experiences as a normal part of a young person's development. Take a show like Euphoria with Zendaya - a show written by teens to represent the teen experience and you will be met with an onslaught of teen sex and exploration. Sex is normal.

Now on the other hand, there's data. An article published by the

Journal of Affective Disorders in 2023 linked early sexual activity and multiple sexual partners to Major Depressive Disorders[12] developing later in life.

Dichotomous? Scandalous? In one hand we hold the world that will encourage you as a young person to explore, lean in, and satiate your sexual desires. On the other hand, there's data that early sexual activity is scientifically linked to Major Depressive Disorders later in life.

Where do we find the truth on sex? Is it something that teens should enjoy and explore as a normal part of a relationship or friendship - or is there a purpose or greater plan for sex?

Where is the truth?

My son Eli is 8, my daughter Selah is 6, and my daughter Amelie is 4. Knowing that as their minds and bodies grow, their understanding of sex is developing as well. Even if they don't have words for it. It was the same with you as well, my friend. Sex, money, friendship, connection, all of those foundational beliefs start so early in tiny experiences. Understanding sex is not one conversation, it's 300 micro-conversations and hundreds of observations about the world around us. My children's sexual identity forms just like the way they see themselves. I want them to observe a few things from me.

1. Dad always comes back to mom
2. Mom and dad share a bed and we do not share the space with others
3. Dad is attracted to mom, loves mom, chooses mom and I like to hug and kiss her

Apart from a physical understanding of the anatomy of sex, my kids are observing that there is something significant, cherished, worth-protecting and it is something my wife and I do not share with others.

Young person, there is something beautiful to be understood about sex. If the truth is that early sexual experiences and multiple partners can be linked to major depressive disorders later in life - we can know the opposite is true as well; there is something powerful within sex, which is the opposite message of what we might get from the rest of the world saying that it's not a big deal and just part of growing up.

We are sexual beings, again, it's inescapable represented in our art forms (music, TV shows, movies, magazines). I want you to feel alive in every aspect of your life. Could it be that there could be *more* life, *more* enjoyment, *more* lasting satisfaction, and eventually *more* freedom by putting some boundaries around our sexual lives as young people? Could sharing this deeply personal part of ourselves with person after person seem like freedom but end up feeling like depression?

Could it be that there is truth out there? Not truth meant to take our freedom but to offer it. A standard, bounds, and authority - and no matter how much effort we put into trying to build our own truths and beliefs or shouting at others "It's my right, it's my truth or I have the right of way" we will find ourselves facing something head-on, you and me, the inevitable oncoming traffic that is the truth.

Green Light.

"Physically dead or the death of a spirit, either way, no I don't want to feel it. These tears of Joy, I'm saying not today - I don't know how but Imma find a way."
– Tae Sosa, Escape.

CHAPTER 52

Bison

I saw a stunning image recently; a massive Bison covered in frost, ice, and snow. It's looming head, an incredible 200 pounds held low and steady over the arctic tundra - face straight into the camera. Dark eyes, indistinguishable in the cold blue frost encompassing it. Like a mountain with a beating heart hidden deep, deep inside.

I learned something very interesting about Bison. When a storm approaches, instinctually they turn their bodies to the storm and run straight into it.

Isn't that wild?

Something about their behavior tugs at my heart as I read more about this incredible fusion of what feels like design, biology, and instinct mixing together.

They run into the snow? Into the rain? Into the wind?

As experts unravel this behavior[13], I learn that Bison know that the quickest way to get through a storm is to face it head on, rather than constantly running from it and finding themselves in the harshest conditions on the edge trying to outrun the storm.

My thoughts immediately surge inward as I overlay this concept into my world and the world that I live in.

The danger of avoidance.
Friend, what do you find yourself running from today? A storm that you must face, a conversation you must have - yet in your avoidance you constantly find yourself on the edges of this storm cell in the harshest of emotional conditions constantly trying to outrun it? You medicate yourself with substances or with never ending self-care. You meditate and get your nails done, you do yoga and breathing exercises, yet nothing saves you from the storm. You are literally self-caring your way into depression.

Bison.

Turn your head, breathe in that arctic air and let it invigorate your lungs, tilt your head down and walk into the storm, my friend. Walk toward the conversation you need to have. Walk into that therapy office to unpack what happened to you. Walk into the storm and like the Bison, may we learn together that the quickest road to peace is walking right into the storm you always felt was chasing you.

> Walk into the storm and like the Bison, may we learn together that the quickest road to peace is walking right into the storm you always felt was chasing you.

CHAPTER 53

Scooters

*"All of us end up somewhere in life, few of us end up
there on purpose."*
– *Craig Groeschel*

I just returned from a walk with my two daughters. It's a few days after Christmas in Michigan and there's no snow. The historic street we live on in the city looks soggy and dreary. I feel this way in my heart today; heavy, gray, foggy, low. I'm hoping that the fresh air and movement will be helpful to me.

You can see your breath, it reminds me of the lyrics we wrote in our song Streetlights *"When every breath starts to float, fading between the warm and the cold."* It's that type of weather.

Both Selah (6) and Amelie (4) received scooters for Christmas, each princess-themed blue and pink and with three wheels as they learn to ride them. Selah takes off in her pink scooter, pink pants, pink sweatshirt, pink hat, pink gloves, and pink shoes. Her bright blonde hair and smile bursts through every moment, she's passionate in everything she does - whether that's riding a scooter, giving a hug, or throwing a fit.

Amelie is having a hard time. Her hair is down today, her strawberry blonde bangs sitting just below her eyebrows enough for her to need to tilt her chin up to see well. She looks a little like a puppy in her tiny cheetah print coat. She shouts ahead to her big sister to wait up. We keep encountering the same problem on our scooter ride, Selah is always 20-30 feet ahead of us and Amelie keeps pushing off with her right leg, gripping her sparkly blue handlebars and veers directly off the sidewalk into the muddy grass. She pushes off, landing her thrusting foot on the sidewalk a few times then hits a landscaping rock, runs into a tree, or down the slope of a driveway towards the street. She picks up her scooter, repositions it towards her big sister down the sidewalk and pushes off again...

...Again, her scooter swerves off the sidewalk into each one of my neighbors' front yards. We are about 20 minutes into our walk down the street and we have not made it to the end of the block. Amelie doesn't know how to steer; she doesn't understand how to lean and shift her weight to adjust her direction. She doesn't know how to turn. She does not know how to get to where she wants to go.

She's 4.

She doesn't understand how the handlebars work apart from something to hold onto and I can see the confusion as she pulls her scooter out of the muddy grass every 8 feet. The only thing she can do is take-off and without the ability to steer, she ends up in the same place. Before we know it, we are both shouting to Selah to wait up for us. It feels like we have been out here for hours, but I can still see my house, we have not gone anywhere.

Some of us will go our whole lives not knowing how to steer. It's not just a 4-year-old issue. Some of us will ride our natural ability to take-off, jump in, get excited about people, money, friendships, school, marriage, careers – we crash, do it again, and wonder why we can never get to where we want to go.

We go from relationship to relationship (crashing) without ever improving who we are as people, never leaning into new skills and cultivating value to bring into a relationship.

We go from job to job excited about the new adventure and earning potential and inevitably quit because every single boss doesn't understand us and is a jerk.

We don't budget, save, or adjust our spending habits and wonder why we are always broke and the world is against us.

We unintentionally sabotage friendships with crippling emotional baggage that we never learn to unpack and work through.

We do not learn to steer. Only take off.

We are constantly running off the sidewalk with Amelie. Together, we constantly smash into rocks and again, pulling our princess scooter out of the mud calling to the people in front of us to wait up!

My dear friend reading this book, what do you keep running into in your life that is ruining opportunity, slowing you down, or creating an unhealthy pattern that keeps you from moving forward? Take a minute to think. Close your eyes, where is your scooter continually swerving off the sidewalk into the grass and mud? There is hope for us, especially if you have learned to ride a scooter or ride a bike - you're already ahead!

Take a minute to think. Close your eyes, where is your scooter continually swerving off the sidewalk into the grass and mud?

If you do not have an answer to what I asked above, I'd encourage you to talk to someone that really loves you. Invite them, with humility, to share with you things in your life that they can see are negatively affecting you over and over again.

My desire for you and for myself is that I we are not only good at taking off. For your friendships, relationships, careers, schooling, bank accounts, and future marriages - I want you to be able to steer.

A good place to start would be journaling about what you would like to experience in life and reflect on if your current decisions are directing you to that place. All of us end up somewhere. Maybe you will reach out to someone ahead of you, grab that princess scooter out of that 4th crashed relationship or 5th crashed job and ask them - how do I do this better? I hate the mud.

CHAPTER 54

Faith Over Feedback

Over anything in life, one of the greatest gifts I can offer to my children is the chance for them to see myself and my wife alive in our passions, chasing dreams, building, and creating.

Often, once kids enter the picture parents can get into the mode of just wanting to make life about supporting the kids, their dreams and passions.

My wife, Heather, is an interior designer (not interior decorator), I have to make that clear. She does not just pick out paint colors and rugs and curtains. She designs bespoke spaces, obliterates walls and erects rooms that the homeowners could not imagine on their own. Dark and moody spaces that bring comfort and a sense of luxury. If you ask my children what their mommy does, they will tell you that she makes homes beautiful. If you ask my kids what I do (their daddy), they will let you know that dad helps makes peoples' hearts feel alive.

Often on Lion Heart tours, my own children will have the chance to come and be part of the team. Eli is 8, Selah is 6, and Amelie is 4 at the time I am writing this. My 4-year-old wants to paint with dad, my son wants to sit next to me or dance before a show in front of the crowd. Their unexpectedness has created some endearing moments during performances.

As my kids grow, one of the things I want them to know is that I am never out of reach, I am never too busy for them. They can always approach me knowing that my arms are open to them. That's why, if I am at a show and my 4-year-old wants to sit next to me and paint or have me pick her up – I will do it. Honestly, it elicits a tangible sense of compassion from the audience and more importantly it shows that I live this with my family. **Focusing on how we develop each other's Identity, self-worth, value, it's not an act or a performance – we live this.** I am just as concerned with my child's sense of worth and value as I am for the 9th grader in the audience, and I believe I can build both. It's the reason I am adamant about making sure to include in our promotional materials that I deliver with a "relaxed polish."

I had just finished a week-long tour in Texas when I received an e-mail on Saturday morning from the coordinator of our tour that week. We had seen upwards of 7,000 students. On the last day, my family flew in, and my children were at the two last shows. This particular school was near and dear to the heart of our coordinator as it was the school that had the most emotional needs and struggles. My son Eli danced prior to the show and the crowd cheered him on, one student even stood up to clap; nodding his head in affirmation and pointing at Eli and offering the most affirming glance and presence. I loved to see that come out of a student. I thanked him in front of the entire audience for having the courage to stand and clap for my small 8-year-old in the way he did. Some people will never experience anyone standing to cheer them on.

My daughter Amelie sat on a stool and painted a corner of the canvas black. She held a microphone like her dad and sang along with the songs in her little voice. Sometimes the audience would let me know if she needed her brush dipped again. I left those shows that day fulfilled. Out of all the performances this week, this specific school got the full picture of who I am, a dad and husband, a performer, artist, singer. They got the full picture.

Historically, my kids have added incredible value to our performances because they are an unexpected variable. With them comes the chance for the audience to see the way I tenderly interact with them with the formation of their identity in mind. I love it.

Back to the email I received. I had just sat down to have breakfast with my kids when I quickly checked my e-mail.

"It was nice to have your family there to cheer you on but having your daughter run in circles around you was inappropriate and sent conflicting messages to the students on expectations to pay attention. I understand the desire to be a good parent and a good performer but today was not one of those times. The school did not get the best of who you are."

I was paralyzed getting this email. In vulnerability and transparency here, my greatest fear is disappointing people and being misunderstood, resulting in losing control of the way people see me. Losing favor with others. It's not healthy and little by little I am chipping away at this insecurity to build into a healthier sense of self.

I couldn't move or respond, my heart raced, I started sweating, my head fell into my hands as I slid my computer over to my wife.

"I feel like she missed the entire picture," I said.
"I literally, thought the shows yesterday were the best of the entire week BECAUSE my kids were there. They got the full *experience* of who I am."

Heather started typing on my computer drafting a response back. The lady who received my response doesn't know (maybe until reading this) that my wife is the one who typed the whole thing and I hit send.

"Good Morning ——————,

Thank you so much for the opportunity. We had a great time, the students and staff were so kind, hospitable, and welcoming. We got to attend a football game at the high school yesterday and connected with a lot of students and staff that expressed tangible stories on how the message impacted them. It was very encouraging. You go all out for Texas football too! Wow, what an experience!

Thank you for taking the time to provide feedback on my family's involvement. I can understand the juxtaposition of being asked to listen, while my daughter was running around and the distraction it may have provided. Fortunately, her running in circles was a small fraction of the assembly and we received a lot of positive feedback from students and staff regarding my kid's presence and the tangible way it connected to the message, like Cam standing up to cheer for my son.

As a former teacher who taught in an overlooked and significantly under-resourced school, many of the students come from broken homes or single parent families. The presence of my kids has historically provided hope for students with a sense of belonging and image of fatherhood they may not have at home – this is a representation of sharing the best of me as a speaker, dad, mentor, and performer. The Lion Heart Experience reflects much more than a single assembly, it is sharing the best of our talents, time, and resources. This is represented by staying after every assembly for hours to connect with students on a deeper level, going to the parade and the homecoming game, hand-written letters to students and staff after the performances, having lunch with students at each school, etc.

In my five years of traveling to schools with The Lion Heart Experience, the feedback of my family's presence has been very positive due to the way it ties in the message in a tangible way. I am thankful my kids not only get to see their dad go to work, but they get to participate in both feeling alive and making others feel alive as well.

I had a teacher pull me aside at the game yesterday who recently lost his father – the assembly was so impactful to him that he left school to visit his sons at their middle school just to tell them he loves them. I was so touched by that story. Another middle school girl came up to me to say hi with her dad and her dad mentioned she has been talking about the assembly all week and listening to the music on repeat. So special!

Thank you again for the feedback and I hope this offers a little bit of perspective on my intentionality behind involving my family. I am so grateful for you and the way you connected us to your community. We hope to see you all again soon!"

Now, why share this with you? Maybe to reveal how fragile I am emotionally;)

No, I share this with you to engrain a phrase into your mind.

Faith over feedback.

Our culture is full of feedback, instant feedback that we receive on everything. Performance reviews, comments, likes, shares. The world is going to give you TONS of feedback. Some of it is going to break your heart. Some of it is going to give you a high you will chase on social media until it makes you sick. But the world is going to offer you feedback up to your ears. Feedback on what you do, how you do it, how you look, why you talk and act that way, how you spend your money and time, what you decide to do with your life. Feedback. Feedback. Feedback.

> The world is going to give you TONS of feedback. Some of it is going to break your heart. Some of it is going to give you a high you will chase on social media until it makes you sick. But the world is going to offer you feedback up to your ears.

The question I'd like to pose for you is this.

Do you have a belief in what you are doing that transcends feedback? Where your belief has turned into a conviction, some type of anchor that you will not let go of. Do you have an unflinching belief in what you do and who you are meant to be that will trump feedback? I do. My desire for my kids to not only see their dad alive and passionate, but to feel welcomed into the whole show and not be treated as an inconvenience or interruption. To have my kids grow up and know I am ALWAYS accessible to them, even if I am in front of 1,000 people. Knowing they can always go up to dad.

This will always be greater than my desire to be loved or accepted by a powerful person or audience.

I have faith in what I feel I am made to do. Who I am made to be, and being an excellent father supersedes all of it.

Young person reading this, my dream for you is to not get swept up in the feedback the world will give you. I hope this for myself too. Maybe the day will come where I get an e-mail like that and there's no mini panic attack for me. My dream for you is that you may catch a glimpse of yourself operating at the intersection of your deepest passions and the world's greatest need. That there your convictions would rest and keep you secure, on a calling to something great and worthy of the best of you.

Around 1907, a young man named Walter sat in his elementary classroom drawing flowers. Each flower had a face.

"Flowers don't have faces,"[14] his teacher said to him, offering scoffing feedback to the artistic expression.

Walt grew up continuing to draw flowers with faces, then a mouse that could sing, then an elephant that could fly. This was Walt Disney. I'm glad he did not listen to the feedback of his elementary school teacher.

My hope for you is that whatever feedback you receive, it would force you to reach down and grip the anchor of your faith in what you are doing. Know I'm here cheering you on. I'm on the road with you.

CHAPTER 55

A Letter to August

"Go ahead and talk to me like you are talking to August," Jackson (my therapist) said to me from across the room. "What do you want to say?"

August was a dear friend of mine that I had personally invested in for the past five years. Early morning coffees and conversation, mentorship, leadership opportunities, encouragement transitioning into marriage and fatherhood from being a single person. I believed in this young man.

A few months prior to this moment with Jackson I was on an evening video call with the board of directors, as well as some key leaders from the non-profit I lead in the city. August was on that call. In late fall, the last bit of leaves had fallen from the trees. Frost began kissing the ground each morning as one season slipped into another. It got dark earlier and earlier in the afternoon.

Inside of me seasons shifted as well, life was dark, and I felt I was hanging on by a thread inside.

This specific evening, I sat on the couch next to my wife Heather and my walker. I was learning to walk again. After eight days and two major surgeries in the hospital removing blood clots that had filled my left leg and lower back, my body and my spirit equalized into a simultaneous broken state. I cannot think of a harder season of my life than what was going to happen this evening.

Frost not only covered the ground, it also covered my soul today. Earlier in the day, before this video call I sat with Jackson, I had gone over two revisions of the talk I was going to make on this evening. Tonight, I was going to step down from leading the non-profit, I was going to bring the reality of my physical and emotional state into the light. I was going to ask if anyone would like to step up in my absence and was also at peace with the work discontinuing if no one did.

My body, reduced by the surgeries was weak and slow and my spirit heavy, burdened and angry. I was not visibly angry, it was deep in my soul, my heart was foaming.

I looked at the screen to see the faces of the board and people important to me that volunteered with the organization present to listen. I read my prepared statement that Jackson helped me refine.

I spoke.

I'm not doing ok right now. I'm learning to walk again. My heart is heavy and burdened and I'm working hard, through therapy to recover and work through all that I am right now. I need a break...

I felt seen and understood by my friends on this call. My friend Jon, who was facilitating this video call said "Joe, it's good that you are working on this now, seeing this now, bringing it up now, at least there has not been a big moral failure or crash. Does anyone else have anything they'd like to say?"

There was silence.

I am not going to lie, I wished deeply that someone on that call said, "Joe, it's brave to speak up and say you are struggling and having a hard time, I'm proud of you." That didn't happen, it would have meant a lot to me.

Note to reader:
If you are ever proud of someone, tell them.

"Actually, I'd like to share," I see movement from the corner of my screen from August – here is a man that I love and believe in. When I look at him, I see morning coffee, conversations about life struggles, I see a companion and teammate.

He continues, "I have been thinking this for two years and I want to bring this up now, there's been significant moral failure under Joe's leadership here..."

August continues, "There's no transparency with finances and decision-making processes, hiring and vetting leaders and I personally know people who are hurt and do not want to be part of this organization because of Joe's leadership and micromanaging."

I was so surprised, hurt, curious, embarrassed all at once. This is someone I have talked to weekly for years and I did not know he felt this way. Secondly, many of the things he brought up I had asked if he would be willing to join our board to help with decision making. He said no.

I had asked for his thoughts and reflections on a recent hire we were struggling with.

I did not want to have sole responsibility over finances. Now all of this was being thrust back into my face as a moral failure.

In an uncharacterized response from me, I was not defensive on the call and asked his forgiveness over zoom for the hurt I caused him and let him know everything he brought up was important to me.

I couldn't sleep for weeks. I had never experienced this type of hurt before. I was sad and angry; I was embarrassed and humiliated.

I got together with August for coffee a few weeks later.

I ordered my regular mocha and everything bagel with cream cheese.

"I thought I had a stronger relationship with you where you may have brought up those conversations to me earlier and in person rather than on a huge call like that," I said.

Knowing his wife was likely offended by my leadership as well, I asked if it would be ok if I reached out to apologize to her.

"No, she just wants to see you change, she just wants to see you get healthy she won't think your apology is sincere. We are actually going to be stepping back to create some distance from you," August responded.

I left that conversation planning in my mind how I would win their trust back, how and when I might be able to prove myself in a healthy state to August and his wife, as well as the other (unnamed) leaders I had hurt.

Note to reader:
I actually recently learned that when someone says, "A lot of us have been talking" and they don't name everyone else, that's called a phantom attack and it's a form of manipulation because you are not able to face your accusers.

I struggled emotionally for months, continually processing the same feelings resulting from this interaction with August. I even brought it up to our marriage counselors, my spirit exasperated and confused, and they told me something I had never once considered in my life.

"It's ok to release the friendship, Joe."

I blinked and froze like a robot trying to process foreign data. What?

Release a friendship? That's not who I am. I'm faithful, I always believe, and I am a good friend.

Our counselor continued, "It's ok to release the friendship and still want the best for them."

I slept and pondered the words for days, looking out the window. Release a friendship?

Days past, so many nights lying awake in bead.

Note to reader:
I'm curious what keeps you up at night. What conversation or interaction are you never able to escape from? I care about that, and I hope this helps you heal.

"Go ahead and talk to me like you are talking to August," Jackson (my therapist) said to me from across the room. "What do you want to say?"
I breathed in slow.

"August, I have loved my time with you, and I have been proud of our friendship. I believe in you and I'm grateful for you - *but* what you did to me on that call, I can't get over it. I do not want to live in a way that I need to prove myself to you. I am going to be done with our friendship."

"That's good, Joe," Jackson said to me with a kind and warm head nod. "You might try getting rid of the 'but,' when you say 'I love you *but*,' it causes the listener to negate everything you just said. Try I love you *and*... hold both realities in both hands at the same time."

I tried again, "August, I have loved my time with you, and I have been proud of our friendship. I believe in you, I'm grateful for my time with you **and** what you did to me on that call was wrong and hurtful. I do not want to live in a way that I need to prove myself to you or anyone, I deserve better. I am going to be done with our friendship."

I left that session emotionally divorced from my connection with August. I've never said those words to him in person. The last conversation I had with him was at Einstein bagel on Woodward Avenue. **The words were for me.**

Leaving the coffee shop being reminded that I needed to prove my health and balance to someone was a reality I had learned was unfair and living to prove yourself to anyone, isn't living.

> In one hand I hold a sincere love and belief in him, with an even more sincere gratitude for my memories with him, and in the other hand I hold something new, a recently found understanding that I deserve better, that it's ok to have standards and boundaries.

This connection with August was my first experience releasing a friendship. In one hand I hold a sincere love and belief in him, with an even more sincere gratitude for my memories with him, and in the other hand I hold something new, a recently found understanding that I deserve better, that it's ok to have standards and boundaries.

Maybe you are reading this today and there's a friendship you must release. Not burn it to the ground, not walk away with your two middle fingers up - just release. It is ok to believe in them, appreciate your time with them, have gratitude for what they have brought in your life, AND acknowledge the hurt they administered crossed a line and that you deserve better.

And after a few months, a touch of frost begins to melt from my soul. I wrote a song called "youknowiloveyoudog" where I say.

"If it all falls apart…you know I love you dog.

Best days are on the way. Even if this doesn't work out, all the memories are safe.

Just remember me with arms wide open and a smile on my face, knowing we'll never be the same, we'll never be the same again… you know I love you dog"

– Joe Vercellino, Youknowiloveyoudog

CHAPTER 56

A Princess Story

I grew up on Disney movies, all of them. *Lion King, Tarzan, Little Mermaid, Aladdin* - their soundtracks are engrained into my DNA. That's part of the reason why I take music writing so seriously, melodies will stay in your mind and body for your whole life. (1) As a parent that's why I sing "When I grow up" and "Lift every voice and sing" to my kids instead of "Rockabye Baby" or "Twinkle, Twinkle Little Star." If they are going to have a melody stuck in their head, I want it to be a life-giving and purposeful melody. (2) We should be mindful and intentional about what we listen to if it's going to become a part of who we are.

> I grew up on Disney movies, all of them. Lion King, Tarzan, Little Mermaid, Aladdin — their soundtracks are engrained into my DNA. That's part of the reason why I take music writing so seriously, melodies will stay in your mind and body for your whole life.

What are the oldest songs you can remember? Maybe it's from a movie or maybe it's the music your parents played in the car or around the house.

I loved, and I mean *really* loved a couple of the staple romantic songs in the Disney movies I'd watch. "Can You Feel The Love Tonight" from *The Lion King*, "A Whole New World" from *Aladdin* and "You'll Be In My Heart" from *Tarzan* were at the top of my

list. I would imagine being able to perform these songs – they just reached the depths of my heart with feeling and passion.
In high school, I went to Disney World with my high school marching band. This was around 2005 (important context for the next part of this story). We marched through Disney, near the castle, and got to record in a Disney recording studio. It made me feel so alive and proud of the group I was with. The last day I wanted to find a CD (yes, a CD, this was before apple music and Spotify if you can believe it). I wanted to find a CD that had all my favorite Disney songs on it. But I didn't want to buy the soundtrack to every movie to listen to on my CD player in my room.

Man, I hate mentioning CD's, because I'm not really that old.

The only problem was that the only CD in the store at Disney that had my favorite songs on it was the Disney Princess Mix. It was a bright, flowery, pink CD with digital graphics of the Disney princesses on it. But it had "A whole new world," "Can you feel the love tonight," and "You'll be in my heart on it."

Reluctantly and slightly embarrassed I took this CD up to the counter to purchase it, knowing exactly what people around me would say when they saw it.

That's so gay! Joe's gay! That's so fruity! If you are a high school student reading this – I'm sure you are familiar with the phase of life that you are in or have passed through where this seemed to be the ultimate burn. If you made it through this phase, congratulations. If you avoided it, props to you. I shake my head now thinking about how dumb and low it is while at the same time, I remember saying I didn't care but actually caring very deep-down what people thought of me.

I just liked the songs.

Before going to bed at night, back in my room at home I would drift off to the sounds of my favorite music. The CD was hidden by the top of my radio so there was no pink to be made fun off.

I'm a 90's kid and if you were a 90's kid you probably had a waterbed. They're 100% trendy, 100% terrible and cold, and 100% amazing.

I had a waterbed, it's all I wanted for Christmas my freshman year - literally a pouch of water held in a rectangle box with sheets, always flowing and bouncing and moving with any touch of movement.

Anyway, I always imagined being able to sing and perform one of these songs someday.

Time went by and my waterbed popped. I went to college and Disney was replaced by Usher and PitBull. No one called me gay for the music I listened to anymore. CDs went away and now all the music you could ever want was on your phone.

I didn't make it into the music program I wanted to in college, wasn't good enough. So, I worked really hard my first year of school to be good enough to get in my second year of school. I sang in coffee shops and on street corners for tips - "a whole new world" settled deep down into my body, hidden with the rest of my childhood songs.

It took me six years to get through college, I failed some classes and somehow managed to get out with a degree. I graduated with a degree in music education and got turned down from a lot of the jobs I applied for. A little school in Detroit hired me because I was good with buckets, trash cans, and drumsticks. I met Tae Sosa at this school.

The next nine years I spent in my classroom creating music with my students that would hopefully one day be the melodies they reminisce on in their adult years.

I started The Lion Heart Experience and left teaching after the COVID-19 pandemic. Five years into our touring around the country I found myself at a high school with The Lion Heart Crew in southwest Michigan.

We had just finished a performance for a few hundred students when a teacher brought up a young girl, probably 15 years old, her hands shook, and her eyes appeared to gaze into the distance while she talked to you in short, fragmented sentences. I did not always understand what she was saying. The teacher mouthed to me that the person who wanted to come up and say hello was on the autism spectrum and was wondering if she could sing with me. "You want to sing with me?" I said to her, in front of the audience. She shook her head heavily up and down and shifted her weight back and forth to motion a cheerful, yes.

Her name was Angela, and she was a sweetheart. I would be lying if I told you I was not a touch hesitant to do this in front of a crowd not knowing what her voice would sound like, considering that she was not able to speak in full sentences.

Nevertheless, I was flowing with this moment as it unfolded.

"What would you like to sing with me today?" I asked her.

"She mouthed something, but I wasn't able to understand, and I looked at the teacher with her for an interpretation…"

"A whole new world, from Aladdin." The teacher said, with an arm around Angela's right shoulder and the other holding her left arm. "She loves that song."

I heard the opening signature piano press through the speakers. Jeremiah, our audio engineer, had already brought the song up and I found myself sitting with Angela in front of a few hundred of her peers curious about what was about to happen.

I felt the lyrics un-earth from my soul as it transported me back to 15 years old.

"I can show you the world, shining shimmering splendid" I sang as my passion for this song came to the surface like blowing dust off of an old box.

"No one to tell us no, or where to go, or say we're only dreaming."

"A whole new world," a velvet and soft voice released into the room from Angela.

"A dazzling place I never knew, but when I'm way up here, it's crystal clear that now I'm in a whole new world with you."

Angela's perceived disability must have allowed her an increase in her musical talent because I was now performing with a flawless Disney Princess.

To quote Rod Wave, *"If I could wrap my arms around this memory, man I would."*

In three minutes, that 15-year-old me walking out of the Disney store with the greatest princess hits CD in my hand, being called gay and fruity, laying on a waterbed thinking about getting to sing this song... He came back to visit for a minute. Tiny little dots and pieces of my youth somewhere out there in the cosmos - all aligned for a moment and then disappeared again for this moment with Angela.

I'm glad I knew every word without having to look at my phone. I'm glad I was able to feel every word and sing with Angela. It was the performance I had forgotten I had dreamed about.

I can still see that little disc spinning in my CD player somewhere in the corner of my mind, pink and white and blue. I can hear it coming to a scratchy and slow stop as I fall asleep. The words and melodies burying themselves deep inside of me - knowing one day they would be brought out one last time.

CHAPTER 57

Season's Greetings

I was on a run through my neighborhood this morning. One mile a day, no more, no less. Don't ask me *"Do you feel like running longer?"* or *"Do you think you will ever want to run a marathon?"* I don't. Ever.

It's so cold and each day I think I'm going to like running a little bit more, but it still hurts. While I was painfully dragging my body along the road in a jog that looks like a jog and moves like a walk - I passed a snowman, he was around my height, probably lived on the shelf at Meijer before enjoying the Christmas season in Detroit. He was a two-dimensional Frosty-looking type snowman, his bright white figure was a stark contrast to the dark browns and faded greens of the winter around him. With a smile he held a sign that said, "Season's Greetings."

I made a sarcastic huff as I jogged past in true Scrooge fashion. I told myself to snap out of it and focus my annoyance on the fact that I couldn't breathe. What's wrong with a season's greeting sign anyway, *what's wrong with me?* I think it reminded me of Christmas cards, you know the ones you get in the mail that have more writing on the outside of the envelope than inside the Christmas card. Man, those cards are so annoying to me. They annoy me because I am such a words-sensitive person. I'd rather get a blank piece of paper from someone that only says, "I'm proud of you, Joe." I don't want a Hallmark card that you just signed, I don't need color or glitter, or a holiday joke. Tell me you love me or that you're proud of me if you are mailing me a card.

I kept thinking on the sign that snowman was holding though… "season's greetings."

Typically, we only use that phrase when we are considering an opening for a holiday card, or we are somewhere between Thanksgiving and Christmas, and we need a start to our company e-mail. Season's greetings comes with a visual as well, doesn't it? *Season's greetings* looks like fresh snow and lights, fireplaces, and wrapped gifts. Season's greetings smells like gingerbread cookies and it feels like a cup of hot chocolate.

Season's greetings, my friend.

Can I expand this phrase for you?

That relationship that ended has left you feeling alone, isolated, and embarrassed. Season's Greetings.

Your job is tough and thankless, you feel discouraged and unseen, and it's been this way for a while. That is a tough season. Season's Greetings.

You are confused on the direction of your life. Everyone seems to have a good idea of what you should do, where you should go, and what to do with your life, except for you. That's a tough season. Season's greetings, my friend.

Your loved one or your friend just passed. It's hard to reconcile and operate in the world without them because they were so important for you. Season's greetings, my dear friend.

Ah, the kiss and greeting of a new season of life.

Young person, would you like to go follow me into the deep end? Would you like to, in this very moment, take a step into maturity that 95% of people

When you sense the season's greetings of a new season of your life — if it a joyous season of celebration, achievement, rest, and fulfillment. Lift up your glass as the season greets you, I'm here to celebrate with you.

your age are not even able to comprehend?

When you sense the season's greetings of a new season of your life - if it a joyous season of celebration, achievement, rest, and fulfillment. Lift up your glass as the season greets you, I'm here to celebrate with you.

If the season's greeting comes and it is cold, lonely, and bleak... if the new season greets you with hardship, lift your head and your glass with me, I'm here to venture through this season with you as well. On the other side of this is a fuller, more alive, more aware, more mature, more appreciative, more resilient version of you I am here to celebrate.

Season's greetings, friend.

CHAPTER 58

Closing Thoughts

Here I stand with you at the end of this book – through my life experiences, through the thoughts and memories, scents, sensations, words spoken, love and intentionality soaked in, large and small cuts and disappointments considered. These stories and observations, glimpses into a world that has shaped my core has left me with who I am. You are all your stories and experiences. When my therapist read my diagnoses to me in the beginning stages of my therapy at 32 years old, general anxiety and pervasive depression; – it became an invitation to me to unpack, consider, take note, and move to heal parts of myself I did not have the tools to address. The process of working through my experiences, thought patterns and beliefs with a professional therapist has lead me to a place in my life where (more than I ever have), I am able to delight in who I am – I am able to offer compassion and understanding to myself in the same way I have extended it to others and I have not always been able to do that.

The world will tell you to celebrate all that you are. Relentlessly.

When we don't understand who we are. When we don't take the time to process things that have happened to us and how it has formed us, what are we celebrating?

> **The world will tell you to celebrate all that you are. Relentlessly.**
>
> **Although well-intentioned, settling there leaves us with the most-shallow form of love**

Although well-intentioned, settling there leaves us with the most-shallow form of love. The kind that looks good on Instagram stories and inspirational posts about our lives – but this shallow love fails us when we are alone with only the person in the mirror at the end of the day.

Maybe it's your turn to pick up a pen.

Consider all that you are.
Take note of what you are.
Inventory all that you are.
Heal parts of who you are.
Work on who you are.
Work through who you are.
Learn who you are.

Then, through this dynamic process of reflection, dialogue, journaling, grieving and note-taking – I will raise my glass with you.

I hope that you discover who you are.

Get to Know Joe

(If you enjoy these questions, check out The Lion Heart Experience App (Dream & Hustle) and fill in your own answers along with the emotional tracker from The Lion Heart Experience)

Current Occupation: Speaker, Teacher, Consultant

Married To: Heather Vercellino, Luxury Interior Designer

Children: Elias, Selah Grace, Amelie

Lives in: Detroit, MI

Education: Bachelor of Music Education, Central Michigan University

Awards: 2021 Detroit Teacher of The Year, *Michigan Department of Education*

Greatest Fear: Being out of control or my children dying.

Favorite Treats: Reese's, Milky Way, BBQ chips, Red Bull, Arnold Palmer

Communication style: Fast, assertive, emotional, I enjoy deep and meaningful conversation.

Most impactful books read:
Cues, Vanessa Van Edwards

Where Do We Go From Here Chaos or Community?, Martin Luther King Jr.

Tattoos On The Heart, Father Gregory Boyle

Why Are All The Black Kids Sitting Together In The Cafeteria, Beverly Daniel Tatum

Rest, Alex Soo-Jung Kim Pang

Live no Lies, John Mark Comer

Outliers, Malcom Gladwell

Crucial Conversations, Patterson, Grenny, McMillan, Switzler

Something I wish people asked me more often:
What are you feeling right now?

Silence, music, or podcasts in the car?:
I like to listen to and share podcasts that I've learned something from. I also really enjoy listening to music while someone is teaching me about the artist in the car.

Place where I am most myself:
Out to eat with my wife and friends – good food, good drinks, and good conversation.

Things I know about myself:
I place a high value on relationships, learning about people is important to me. I love to give and be generous, it is one of the best parts of my personality. I am very intentional with my words and actions. I am a dreamer and a visionary. I think generationally about my decisions, gifts and actions. I need to be around passionate people to survive. My best friends Dream & Hustle* I love physical touch and a hand on my shoulder or telling me you are proud of me means a lot to me.
Dream & Hustle attributed to Jeremiah Kanneth

Things that upset me:
Being misunderstood and feeling unappreciated

I feel most balanced when I am:
Around water, not hungry, when I have done something for my heart, soul, mind, and strength by the end of the day.

My mornings go best:

When I am not rushed, if I can wake up a little early. Light a candle, be still and read, sit on the couch.

My last thought before going to sleep:
I breathe in deep and try to visually scroll my whole day into that breath inside my mind. Then I exhale and say "thank you" slowly for all the experiences of the day.

My first thought waking up:
I wish I could sleep longer, always.

Bring it up or hold it in:
If there's an issue, I will bring it up quickly or it will throw me off for the whole day. Especially relational tension or conflict.

What's most important to me:
This has shifted a lot in my life. Currently, being proud of who I am at the end of the day is important to me. Ending my day with my wife, talking, and having a glass of wine on the couch.

My favorite phrases that reflect my beliefs as a person.

A penny saved is a penny
*Phrase attributed to Quicken Loans (Detroit, MI)

If you are more old school, you might have finished that with "a penny saved is a penny earned." You don't get rich by clipping coupons, although I believe in saving. I believe **more** in creating value, taking risks, and getting that value out into the world in a way that people pay for what you bring.

Take the roast out of the oven
*Phrases attributed to Quicken Loans (Detroit, MI)

If you've ever cooked a roast, sometimes it can stay in the oven for 8+ hours. The general idea is that the longer it cooks slowly, simmering in the low heat and juices that the better it's going to taste. The truth is that after a certain point, it doesn't really matter, the roast that's been in the oven for 10 hours tastes the same as the roast that's been in the oven for 12. ***Take the roast out of the oven*** challenges me when I have a creative idea I am constantly working on, tweaking, adjusting, revamping until I think it's perfect. The truth is that there is a point where the quality is not really changing much, time to take the roast out of the oven. Get your idea, your art, your song, your publication out there into the world and move on to the next great idea. In a way, this book is an expression of this belief. I decided I would write for six months and publish whatever I had.

Something's going to happen

Originally coined by the most laid-back and non-anxious friend of mine, Tony. He would always say this around me whenever I was anxious about not knowing what was going to happen. I have a tendency to want to control things around me. Outcomes, environments, places. I do not like to feel out of control. If I was ever around Tony and I said something like "I don't know what's going to happen," he would respond with "well, something is going to happen." It's always been a gentle reminder to me that in the unknown, something will happen - and like the last thing that happened - I will probably make it through.

I'm ok, my body is uncomfortable

This was a phrase my therapist Jackson taught me to say to myself when I started feeling the effects of anxiety and physical pain. I learned to take breaths and try my best to separate my state of being with what was happening to me physically. (deep breathe in and out) "I am ok." (deep breath in and out) "My body is uncomfortable."

Favorite Quotes:

My favorite quote is from the movie "Beasts of The Southern Wild," a poetic telling of a young girl in the New Orleans bayou, who's community suffers a massive flood and she lives with her dad in a floating bathtub.

1. *"When it all goes quiet behind my eyes, I see everything that made me lying around in invisible pieces. When I look too hard, it goes away. And when it all goes quiet, I see they are right here. I see that I'm a little piece in a big, big universe. And that makes things right..."* - Hushpuppy, *Beasts of The Southern Wild*

This quote always offers me perspective on my life. I am the accumulation of so many experiences, people, words, dreams, love, embarrassments, failures, successes. Those pieces are all right there around me, constantly, when I look too hard, they disappear but I always am aware of their presence. In the end, many have come before me and many will come after. I'm a tiny piece in a big story; important, but still tiny.

2. **"It might not be ok, but you could be"** - Lauren Bongiorno, MA, LPC, NCC

I sat down and talked to a teen therapist about her job and asked, "At the end of the day, do you feel like it's just your job to let people know it's all going to be ok?" She responded in a beautiful way "No, because you cannot tell people it's all going to be ok. Most times it actually might not turn out ok, it might be terrible..." My eyebrows raised, thinking about all the times I told people "It's all going to be ok." Turns out it was bad advice!

"But you... *you* could be ok," she said with a smile. "And that is where I do my best work with teens, helping them understand that they can survive, grow, mature, and learn. It might not be ok, but they could be."

3. **"Let the world feel the weight of who you are and let them deal with it"** - author unknown

4. **"You don't have to light yourself on fire to keep other people warm."** - Jackson Morehead MA, LPC, LLP, RN

This quote hits right where it needs to if you are anything like me. You don't need to ruin your emotional life, pour yourself out, exhaust yourself, always say yes, or take all the responsibility to keep others happy.

References

1. Clay, R. (2023, January 1). Suicide Prevention Gets a New Lifeline. American Psychological Association. https://www.apa.org/monitor/2023/01/trends-suicide-prevention-lifeline

2. (2023, March 8). Centers for Disease Control and Prevention. Children's mental health data and statistics. https://www.cdc.gov/childrensmentalhealth/data.html

3. Meet the Press. (2023, December 31). More than 50,000 Americans died by suicide in 2023, more than any year on record [Video]. NBC News. https://www.nbcnews.com/meet-the-press/video/more-than-50-000-americans-died-by-suicide-in-2023-more-than-any-year-on-record-201161285832

4. Centers for Disease Control and Prevention. (2023, February 13). U.S. Teen Girls Experiencing Increased Sadness and Violence [Press release]. https://www.cdc.gov/nchhstp/newsroom/2023/increased-sadness-and-violence-press-release.html

5. Leland, J. (2022, April 20). How Loneliness Is Damaging Our Health. The New York Times. https://www.nytimes.com/2022/04/20/nyregion/loneliness-epidemic.html

6. Trinko, K. (2018, May 3). Gen Z: The Loneliest Generation? USA Today. https://www.usatoday.com/story/opinion/2018/05/03/gen-z-loneliest-generation-social-media-personal-interactions-column/574701002/

7. Bakhtiari, K. (2018, May 3). Gen Z is the Loneliest Generation, And It's Not Just Because Of Social Media. Forbes. https://www.forbes.com/sites/kianbakhtiari/2023/07/28/gen-z-the-loneliness-epidemic-and-the-unifying-power-of-brands/?sh=6011306a6790

8. Rogel Cancer Center. "Normal Ovarian Function." *Rogel Cancer Center | University of Michigan*, Feb. 2014, www.rogelcancercenter.org/fertility-preservation/for-female-patients/normal-ovarian-function.

9. NPR. (2023, January 13) The Transformative Power of Awe. https://www.npr.org/2023/05/06/1174476949/transformative-power-of-awe

10. Benson, K.: The Secret Weapon of Emotionally Connected Couples. The Gottman Institute. Repair https://www.gottman.com/blog/repair-secret-weapon-emotionally-connected-couples/

11. Feinstein, J. (2023, February 16). His Army-Navy Fumble Left Him 'Devastated.' He Still Isn't Over It. The Washington Post. https://www.washingtonpost.com/sports/2023/02/16/anton-hall-army-navy-fumble/

12. Staloch, L. (2023, July 8). New Study Finds a Causal Link Between Sexual Activity Early In Life And Major Depressive Disorder. PsyPost. https://www.psypost.org/2023/07/new-study-finds-a-causal-link-between-sexual-activity-early-in-life-and-major-depressive-disorder-166201

13. "The Bison Advantage." *National Bison Association*, bisoncentral.com/the-bison-advantage/.

14. Korkis, Jim. "The Education of Walt Disney." *Mouseplanet.com*, 4 May 2022, mouseplanet.com/the-education-of-walt-disney/8273/.